Elizabeth Jane Whately

The gospel in Bohemia

Sketches of Bohemian religious history

Elizabeth Jane Whately

The gospel in Bohemia
Sketches of Bohemian religious history

ISBN/EAN: 9783337283445

Printed in Europe, USA, Canada, Australia, Japan

Cover: Foto ©Lupo / pixelio.de

More available books at **www.hansebooks.com**

THE GOSPEL IN BOHEMIA.

Sketches of Bohemian Religious History.

BY

E. JANE WHATELY,

AUTHOR OF "HOW TO ANSWER OBJECTIONS TO REVEALED RELIGION,"
"COUSIN MABEL'S EXPERIENCES," ETC.

LONDON :
THE RELIGIOUS TRACT SOCIETY.
56 PATERNOSTER ROW, 65 ST. PAUL'S CHURCHYARD,
AND 164 PICCADILLY.

PREFACE.

Iɴ introducing the following sketches of Bohemian Religious History to the reader, I must premise that it is not the object of the present work to give a full and complete history of the country, either political or religious. Such an undertaking would require far more research and far more abundant materials than in the present case it is possible to bestow and to obtain.

The aim of the work before us is much simpler and more circumscribed. Happening to meet, some years ago, with an old chronicle much prized by the Moravian Church on the Continent, I thought that the substance of its narrative would be interesting and valuable, and probably new to most readers, and accordingly made an abridged and free translation of the principal part.

The *Persecutions-büchlein*, or Book of Persecutions, as the original document is entitled, is a history of the sufferings endured by the followers of the pure gospel in Bohemia, from the first introduction of Christianity in the Middle Ages, to the final defeat of the Protestants by the armies of the Emperor Ferdinand II. It is supposed to have been drawn up and compiled under the superintendence of Amos Commenius, the celebrated bishop and writer of the Bohemian Brethren's Church; it was written originally in Latin, by certain pious members of the Church, and was translated into German by Bernard Czermenka. It has been freely rendered, to make the narrative more clear and interesting to modern readers; and with the same view some redundancies, amplifications, and lengthened comments on the incidents related have been omitted as unsuitable to the taste of the present day. Some histories of remarkable judgments have also been omitted, from the fear that they might give an air of romance to the whole. They were certainly credited at the time; but it is very possible that in periods of terrible distress and agitation, the excitement of men's minds may have caused their imaginations to magnify trifling incidents, and made them too ready to discern supernatural interferences without sufficient reason.

With the exception of these omissions, the narrative is faithfully reproduced. The papers first appeared in the *Family Treasury;* and are now brought out in a separate form, with some additions, partly to furnish explanations and fill up blanks, and partly to bring down the narrative, as far as possible, to the present day. For the former, I am much indebted to the works of Mr. Hardwicke on the Church of the Middle Ages, and Mr. Pattison on the History of Evangelical Christianity. Bost's *History of the Moravians*, published by the Religious Tract Society, also affords much information respecting the origin and history of the "Brethren's Church." The additions to the narrative subsequent to the date of the Chronicle are gathered from the materials kindly lent by members of the Moravian Church. These details are but scanty; but this is the inevitable result of the circumstances of the case. The record is one of a country in which political and religious liberty were crushed almost at a single blow by the iron hand of a relentless despotism, and the voice of truth was silenced till its very existence in the country was almost forgotten by the rest of the world.

It is the record of a history which has scarcely a parallel in the world's annals; the history of the death and resurrection of the oldest *pure* and Evangelical community existing, with the sole exception of the Waldenses—a community kept alive for centuries in the midst of a furnace of persecution, then apparently crushed to death, and then arising with new life from the ashes, to win triumphs for the gospel among the heathen.

Such a record of "life from the dead" cannot but strengthen the faith of Christian readers ; and if any should be led to study the subject further, or still more to realize more intensely the faithfulness of Him whose promises are "yea and amen" to His people, these pages will not have been compiled in vain.

E. JANE WHATELY.

THE GOSPEL IN BOHEMIA.

INTRODUCTORY CHAPTER.

THOSE who have looked from the fortress-like heights of the Saxon Switzerland, and seen the fair land of Bohemia spread out before them with its forest-covered hills and green valleys, will have been struck, not only with its beauty, but with the peculiar character of the country. Set in, like a picture in a frame, with mountains on all sides, it seems as if intended to stand alone, independent among the countries of Central Europe. The countenance and language of the people, distinctively Slavonic, among so many German provinces, seem to point out the country as one isolated from its neighbours.

But the fate of Bohemia has been involved, in a remarkable manner, in the history of surrounding nations. Few countries have had a sadder or more eventful history—a history peculiarly interesting to the Christian reader, as being especially connected with the spread of gospel truth in spite of serious hindrances and perils.

The Chronicle, an abridgment of which we now offer to our readers, commences with the first establishment

B

of Christianity in the country; but the records of that early time are sadly meagre and imperfect.

Indeed it is noteworthy how very scanty are the details we possess relative to a subject so interesting to all Christians in our own country and on the Continent, as the evangelization of the central, north-eastern, and northern parts of Europe, including in these last our own British Isles.

This arises partly from circumstances in the history of the Christian Church. The first triumphs of the Gospel were rapid as well as lasting: the command, "Go ye into all the world, and preach the Gospel to every creature," was promptly obeyed by the apostles; and in their lifetime the blessed message had been rapidly proclaimed through Western Asia, Greece, and Italy.

But in the next ages the outward progress was slower. For the first three centuries the Church had to hold her ground through fierce storms of persecution; and when at last Christianity became dominant in the reign of Constantine, its pristine purity was already on the wane. The line of demarcation between the Church and the world grew fainter in prosperous days; and too many of the remaining true-hearted disciples, who might have been "the light of the world," were led by the growing spirit of monasticism to hide that light in the seclusion of a hermitage or a convent.

Then came the fall of Rome and the fearful incursions of hordes of barbarians from the north. But out of this terrible evil good was to spring: a new element was infused into the worn-out life of the empire, and among the wild races of northern barbarians the future of Europe lay.

In the midst of the darkness and confusion which attended the close of the old Roman empire and the rise and progress of fresh nationalities, the Church still held on her way; and though she was debased by many corruptions and by the increasing power of a worldly hierarchy, the lineaments of genuine Christian life may be traced, and witnesses for the gospel discovered, in the darkest times.[1]

But the very existence of Christianity as an orthodox confession of faith was imperilled again and again; the terrible persecutions by the Arian Vandals in North Africa, and afterwards the rise of Islamism, threatened to destroy the feeble life, and would have been successful had it not been sustained through all adverse influences by a higher power.

Looking on all these external adverse circumstances, and on the additional hindrance of constant disputes within the Church, we can hardly wonder that it was not till the seventh century was far advanced that any effective and persevering efforts were set on foot for evangelizing Northern and Central Europe.

It is in or about the seventh century that we trace the commencement of the powerful missionary movement which characterised the period intervening between that century and the tenth. Imperfectly as in many respects it was carried on, and much as the growing monastic spirit marred its purity, it was still a noble work, and forms the brightest spot in those dark days. But the troublous character of the times, the scarcity of literary attainments, and the consequent difficulty of preserving records of work, make it nearly impossible to collect anything like a clear and con-

---

[1] See Neander's *History of the Early Church.*

nected history of the European Missions of the Middle
Ages.

We know that in the seventh century the Irish
evangelist Columbanus, with his countryman Gallus,
planted the gospel in Swabia and Switzerland; that in
the eighth century the English Boniface laboured in
Germany; that the ninth was marked by the labours of
Anskar, the apostle of the north, in Scandinavia and
North Germany; and that at nearly the same time, the
gospel was first preached among the numerous and
important branches of the Slavic or Slavonian race.
This extensive family of mankind, extending from the
Elbe to the Don on the east, from the Baltic to the
Adriatic southwards, had remained almost ignorant of
Christianity till the beginning of the ninth century.

It is worthy of notice that there appears to be a
certain analogy between the early history, respectively,
of the Slavic nations in the east of Europe and the
Keltic in the west. Both races were to a certain extent
overwhelmed by the more powerful Teutons; but, on the
other hand, the two weaker races had certain elements
wanting in the stronger, by which the latter seem to
have been influenced and modified. But the subject is
too large to be more than touched on here.

It was a remarkable feature in the early evangelization of both the Keltic and Slavic races, that they were
originally far more independent of the influence of
Rome than the Germanic tribes, whether in England or
on the Continent. In our own country the influence
of the Irish and Scotch missionaries, though largely
thwarted by the pretensions of Rome, predominated in
the north; while the authority of Rome was acknowledged in the south. The struggle was a protracted

one, and ultimately the Roman power gained the ascendency; but, in Ireland especially, it was long before it was entirely established.

In the Slavic part of Europe the struggle began quite as early and lasted longer.

The first effort made for the evangelization of these regions was in 800, by Amo, Archbishop of Salzburg; another was subsequently made by Hrolf, Archbishop of Lorch and Bishop of Passau. Through their agency the first mission was begun in the Slavonian country of Moravia, then governed by an independent king; but little progress was made till about 861–863, or, as the Chronicle states, 894, when two brothers, priests of the Greek Church, Cyrillus and Methodius, arrived to carry on the work.

It is recorded in the *Annals of Nestor* (the most ancient of the Slavonian chroniclers), that the Moravian princes Rotislav, Swiatopolk, and Kotzel, sent to the Emperor Michael III. at Constantinople, requesting him to send them teachers who would instruct them and their people in the Scriptures. On conferring with the Greek clergy, they recommended him to send the two brothers; Methodius, on account of his knowledge of the Slavonian language; Cyrillus, because he was well acquainted with several oriental languages.

Whether they constructed the Slavonian alphabet is doubtful; but it is certain that they translated the Psalms, the Gospels, and other portions of the Scriptures into Slavonic. This important work was accomplished to the great satisfaction of the Slaves; for, says Nestor, "the Slavonians rejoiced on hearing the greatness of God related in their own tongue." That these missionaries were actuated by a truly Christian, rather than a mere ecclesiastical, spirit, is manifest not only in the dissemination of Scripture truth, but also in their disregard of the prejudice which represents the common language of a people as too profane to be employed for sacred uses, and in the employment of the vernacular in public worship. They naturally introduced among their converts the rites of the Eastern Church, but at the same time they recognised the supremacy of the pope. In spite of numerous obstacles they proclaimed the gospel, ordained priests, and administered the sacraments, not only in Moravia, but also in Bohemia, and were very successful in the conversion of many from paganism to Christianity.

But the work was hindered by the jealousy which existed between the Greek and Latin Churches; and it was found necessary for the missionaries to go to Rome to come to an understanding with the pontiffs. They did this about six years after their arrival in Moravia.

From this time we lose sight of Cyrillus, who either died or entered a convent (about 871–873); but Methodius was consecrated by the Pope Metropolitan of Moravia, and returned to resume his missionary labours. He was not long allowed to prosecute them in peace; for his attachment to the Greek ritual and his constant use of the Slavonian language excited the displeasure of his German fellow-labourers. He went again to the pope (in the year 879), by the desire of the latter, to plead his own cause, and actually succeeded in convincing the pontiff of the soundness of his doctrinal views, and of the propriety of conducting worship in the language of the people: for the general use of Latin was only beginning to creep in. On this point the pope actually defended Methodius; he also confirmed him in his archbishopric of the Moravian Church, with powers of administration independent of all other ecclesiastical authorities and responsible only to the see of Rome.

Methodius returned to his work in Moravia; and it was at this time, as will be noticed in the Chronicle, that he appears to have been instrumental in the conversion of Borcziwoi, the Duke of Bohemia, the vassal and guest of the King of Moravia. He continued his labours amid much opposition, is said to have completed the translation of the Scriptures, went again to Rome about 881, and was either forbidden to return to his see or died soon after.

The struggles between the Germano-Romish and Slavo-Greek factions appear to have seriously retarded the progress of the gospel in Moravia. The king of that country was ultimately defeated, and the independence of his kingdom destroyed, by the Bohemian and Hungarian armies; and from this time the religious history of Bohemia and Moravia may be looked on as one,—the Bishop of Bohemia being head of the Churches in both countries.

Meanwhile the struggle between Christianity and heathenism in Bohemia, as we see in the Chronicle before us, was long and severe. In 950, the heathen duke, Boleslav the Cruel, was defeated by the Emperor Otho I., and the accession of Boleslav the Pious in 967 established Christianity on a firm footing.

The bishopric of Prague (the capital of Bohemia) was founded in his lifetime; it was filled in 983 by a learned German, Adalbert. Noted for his missionary zeal, he laboured with the king's help to extirpate the remnants of paganism. But his measures were too hasty and harsh; and this, with the dislike of the people to anything German, soon compelled him to resign his post. In 994, the Roman Synod ordered him to resume his functions, and he reluctantly returned to Bohemia, but was soon again rejected. He finally died a martyr in 997, while seeking to convert the Prussians in the neighbourhood of Dantzig. Neander gives some interesting details concerning this faithful evangelist, who, though intolerant, and sometimes too vehement and harsh, seems to have had an earnest and zealous missionary spirit.

In 966 the gospel passed from Bohemia to Poland. A Bohemian princess, Dombrovka, was married to the Duke of Poland, Mieczyslaw; and, like the pious wife of Clovis, and our English Bertha, she was the means apparently of converting her husband and introducing Christianity. Like Boleslav the Pious, the Polish duke injured his cause by his intemperate violence in suppressing pagan worship; but eventually the new religion was firmly established.

In all these Slavic countries, the establishment of Christianity was closely followed by the attempts of the Church of Rome to force the Latin ritual on the people; and in every case it was combated. Between 1030 and 1058, great efforts were made in Poland and Bohemia to bring the people to acquiesce in the western customs; and gradually the Romish liturgy made its way; but the love of their own ritual was never entirely extirpated; and indeed we may date from this time the commencement of that struggle in Bohemia which only ended with the fatal battle of the White Mountains, in the seventeenth century.

The outline of this long and important struggle is given in the Chronicle before us; but a few preliminary words may be needed to make the general drift of the narrative clearer, and to supply omissions.

The traces of this history are marked by the blood of many martyrs ; but it would not be correct to affirm that the struggle was wholly a religious one. Political and national feelings had a very large share in it. The Slavonic races were passionately attached to their own language, habits, and institutions ; and having been first converted by members of the Greek Church, the colour of their religious feelings, so to express it, was very much taken from the Greek ritual.

The German races, on the other hand, had all more or less yielded, like the Romance peoples of the south, to the influence of Rome. The national feelings of the Slavonians were therefore enlisted in the struggle, and led them to resist German influence, and cling fondly to their own liturgy and language ; and doubtless numbers took that side in the struggle, moved only by national affections and prejudices.

Neither must it be too hastily assumed that the early opponents of Rome were what we should call enlightened reformed Christians. The light of gospel truth came very slowly. At first (as already observed) worship in their native tongue was the chief point contended for ; but afterwards the emissaries of Rome sought to introduce popish ceremonies, to prohibit the marriage of the clergy, to refuse the cup to the laity in the observance of the Lord's Supper. These innovations were strenuously opposed ; and, one after another, preachers were raised up, who (like Savonarola in Italy) inveighed against the corruption of morals among the laity and clergy, and especially the latter. Milicz and his successor, Matthias, who will be further alluded to in the Chronicle, were among the chief of these. They did not attack Romish doctrines as Wycliffe did: but they paved the way for more direct teaching, both by exposing the practices of the Romish clergy, and by dwelling on the necessity for heart repentance and faith in Christ, rather than on the importance of outward ceremonial.

Matthias thus writes of Christ as the only Mediator: " If thou pourest out thy soul to any one in warm feeling and words, as if wishing to find the crucified Jesus, thou wilt depart from him embittered in mind, finding in thyself that thou hast there lost the grace of Jesus Christ, and thy toil and fine words as well. Thus neither wilt thou venture, openly and solemnly, to confess Christ crucified, because then thou wilt, without scruple, be treated as a heretic, and wilt not depart unreviled or unspat upon: and then, by experience, thou wilt feel this exceeding great tribulation and most bitter experience of all faithful bodies, consciences, and souls in Jesus."[1]

Thus these teachers prepared the way for the next witness to the truth, JOHN HUSS.

Huss was born in 1373, and began life evidently as a devout Romanist; but the works of Wycliffe exerted a powerful influence on his mind, and when exhorted to condemn them, he replied, " I wish my soul may be where that excellent Briton is !"

But though he loved and honoured the English preacher, he was far from being equally advanced in his convictions. At first he thought the opinions of Wycliffe too daring, and not without danger; but the

---

[1] Pattison's *Evangelical Christianity.*

more he studied them the more assured he was that they were in harmony with the Scriptures.

Like many other witnesses for Christ in the middle ages, he preached faithfully gospel doctrines, which, though nominally admitted, had been practically denied or ignored by the Romish teachers. In all ages, but especially at this period, there were many who, while devoutly attached to the Church of Rome, did at the same time preach and inculcate a full reliance on the finished work of Christ and union with Him through a living faith. In the words of a living writer:

"All through the dreary ages when the scholastic philosophies employed, in·fruitless questions, the intellects and leisure of the learned, there is to be found in their writings, hid under a mass of rubbish, an acknowledgment of the necessity of accepting the doctrine of Christ's merit in atoning for sins."

The gospel was there, underlying much that might be termed "wood, hay, and stubble;" and in many instances it was not only held and practised, but faithfully and earnestly preached.

To this class of gospel Christians Huss originally belonged; and but for the bitter persecution of the Romish Church, he might never have been known as an opponent of her doctrines.

At the time when his influence was first becoming powerful and general, from his discourses in the Bethlehem chapel, Prague (of which he was nominated minister in 1400), his "orthodoxy," in the Romish sense, was unimpeachable; we find him bearing a commission from the Primate Sbynco, and conducting an inquiry into the genuineness of a reputed miracle at Wilsnack.[1]

[1] See Hardwicke's *History*.

But his indignation at the degeneracy and corrupt morals of the clergy eventually alienated Sbynco, who, imputing the sensation produced to the spread of Wycliffe's tracts, ordered them to be collected and burnt. The pope, Alexander v., was appealed to in 1409, and an interdict was obtained from Rome forbidding Huss to preach in the Bethlehem chapel. To this Huss paid no heed. On his protesting against the conduct of the primate and his clergy, he was charged with heresy, and summoned to appear before Pope John XXIII. He, however, did not deem it safe to obey the summons. The King and Queen of Bohemia were Huss's supporters; but the pope issued a sentence of excommunication against him, or this failing, a command to appear at Bologna to answer for himself.

The archbishop, however, was reconciled to him through the mediation of the king and queen; but in 1412 Sbynco died, and, as mentioned in the Chronicle, Pope John's traffic in indulgences called forth the vehement denunciations of Huss and his friend Jerome. The latter lost no time in propagating his enthusiasm among the students, who, in order to exact a kind of vengeance for the seizure of Wycliffe's writings, organized a mock procession in the streets of Prague, and burnt the papal instruments.

It appears that this violence alienated the king from Huss; and, although he had not himself sanctioned the irregularity, and afterwards regretted its occurrence, the most formidable censures of the Church alighted on his head. He could no longer prosecute his public missions, but addressing an appeal to Jesus Christ Himself, the only righteous judge, retreated from the theatre of strife and lived in retirement in his native village. He there occupied himself with writing defences of the doctrines of Wycliffe, and exhorting the crowds who flocked to hear him to rely on the Scriptures alone as their rule of faith.

In his principal work, the *Tractatus de Ecclesiâ*, he insists on the fact that Christ, and He alone, is the Head of the Church, but also urges the importance of obeying the pope and cardinals "as long as they teach the truth according to the law of God." "The works which Huss composed in his retirement," says Hardwicke, in his *Church History of the Middle Ages*, "have enabled us to mark the final stages in the growth of his belief. To many of the characteristic dogmas then prevailing in the Church he yielded his unwavering assent, confining his denunciations mainly to those points which he regarded as excrescences, abuses, or distorted forms of truth. His principles, indeed, had they been logically apprehended and consistently applied, must have constrained him to relinquish some of the positions advocated by the western schoolmen; but, unlike his English fellow-worker, Wycliffe, Huss had not been largely gifted with the logical faculty, and therefore he continued all his life unconscious of his own divergencies. So far was he, indeed, from meditating the formation of a sect, that he had hoped to renovate the Western Church entirely from within.

A reference to these facts may well explain the readiness he showed to vindicate himself before the Council of Constance, whither he was now summoned to proceed. That great assembly constituted in his eyes the lawful representative of Christendom; and as he had no longer any hope of finding justice at the papal court, he went in search of it elsewhere. We see him starting for the council (October 11, 1414), armed with testimonials of his 'orthodoxy' from the Primate of Bohemia and the titular Bishop of Nazareth, who was officiating as the inquisitor of the heresy in the diocese of Prague. He also bore the passport or safe conduct of Sigismund, King of the Romans (and afterwards emperor), which guaranteed his personal protection in the strongest terms."

This promise was deliberately violated, on the pretext, alleged by the council, that Huss, by impugning the orthodox faith, had rendered himself an outcast from all privileges, as promises of safety were only binding when made to those who kept the Catholic faith.

We all know the subsequent history; how he reached Constance, attended by a band of faithful friends and adherents, and how his enemies in Bohemia, who had been labouring to counteract and repress his work, had found means of arriving before him and poisoning the minds of his judges. Palecz, his former colleague in the university of Prague, was one of his bitterest enemies and most unscrupulous calumniators; Huss, then, found many of the council already prejudiced against him, and fell an easy prey to their machinations. He was taken into custody and kept for nearly eight months in prison.

The report of his verbal answers in his examination, even as given by his enemies, and the tracts he wrote in prison, show that in almost every point he held the same views as those professed by some of the members of the council before whom he stood as a criminal. They agreed with him in their desire to reform the clergy and retain the papal power; but their strong national prejudice against him as a Bohemian, and their horror of Wycliffe, whom he would not condemn (though he was far less advanced than the great English reformer), overcame all other considerations, his doctrines were condemned as heretical, and, as he would not recant, he was condemned to perish at the stake.

The history of that last condemnation is generally known. A darker page in the annals of Romish persecution scarcely exists. On July 6, 1415, the council assembled to pronounce sentence. The emperor came in great state, and accompanied by the princes of the empire and many of the nobility; cardinals, bishops, priests, and doctors appeared in large numbers. The Bishop of Lodi preached on the extirpation of heresy and heretics, closing with an appeal to the emperor to destroy Huss. The accusation against the reformer was then read, but reply was forbidden. Sentence was then pronounced, and immediately put into execution. He was first degraded from his priestly office, the vestments were put upon him, and when he was completely habited, the bishops removed the cap and robes one after the other with maledictions and insults. The mark of the tonsure was then cut from his head, and his finger-nails were scraped with a knife. He was thus formally degraded from the service of the Church, and having been delivered up " to Satan and to hell," he was handed over to the secular arm.

The executioner and his assistants at once led him to the stake, where he and everything he had about him was burnt. But nothing could shake his calm and majestic patience. He felt that nothing could separate him from the true Church of Christ, and his last breath at the stake was spent in singing a hymn of praise to

God. His ashes were flung into the Rhine, that nothing might remain on earth of so execrable a heretic.

His enemies now turned to his companion and friend Jerome of Prague, to wreak their relentless fury on him. Ardent and enthusiastic as he was, his courage failed for a moment, and he consented to recant; but it was only a temporary weakness; he recalled his abjuration publicly and boldly, and was handed over to the secular power. As he went to the place of execution he repeated the Apostles' Creed; at the stake he told his executioner to light the pile before his face, for had he been afraid of the fire he would not have been there now.

In the very flames he was heard chanting the Easter hymn, and his heavenly joy struck even his bitterest enemies.

When the tidings of the execution of the martyrs reached their own country, hostility to the Germans and to Sigismund broke out openly, and a revolutionary war, which lasted for thirteen years, and was attended with ferocious cruelties, commenced. The administration of the cup in the Lord's Supper to the laity, on which Huss himself, though he practised it, seems to have laid less stress than his disciples, was taken up vehemently by several of his successors, and especially by Jacob of Mirs; as early as the autumn of 1414 this teacher had begun to lay especial stress on this usage. The other side was taken by the Council of Constance, and the "chalice" grew into a watchword of that numerous party in Bohemia who revered the memory of Huss.

For several years the Hussite party kept the forces of the empire at bay; but their religious differences were fatal to their cause. The moderate party, called Calixtines and Utraquists, from *calix*, a cup, and *utraque*, both (referring to communion in both kinds), adhered to Huss and Jacob Mirs, claiming that the word of God should be freely preached in the country, the communion administered with both bread and wine, and strict discipline enforced.

But the more extreme party, called Taborites, from Tabor (a camp), the name given to a Bohemian mountain where they first held their religious meetings, and afterwards pitched their camp, were much more determined and persevering in their resistance.

Under the renowned General John Ziska (who seems, however, to have been more of a political than a religious hero) they gained brilliant victories. At one time Sigismund suffered so large a loss of men that he was not unwilling to accede to a truce, and make the following concessions :—1. That Divine service should be conducted in the vernacular ; 2. That the Lord's Supper should be observed with both bread and wine ; 3. That the clergy should have no secular jurisdiction ; 4. That violations of morality should be punished as severely as breaches of the criminal laws.

But this did not continue long. In the end the Taborites were suppressed by the Bohemian Government, and after the middle of the fifteenth century they disappear as a political body. From this extreme section, when the fierce and fanatical element had been eliminated, there sprang eventually that venerable Church of the Brethren of Bohemia, which, jointly with the kindred Church of the Waldenses, upheld gospel truth through the darkest ages of bigotry and superstition.

C

A sketch of this ancient Church, which links the memory of Huss and Jerome of Prague on one side, with the honoured missionary labours of the Moravian Church of our own days on the other, is given in the Chronicle to which these pages are an introduction. There will necessarily be some repetition at first, but it was needful to go over the same ground in order to give some explanations of points only slightly touched on by the writer of the Chronicle.

CHAPTER I.

THE conversion of the Bohemians to Christianity is supposed to have taken place in the year 894.[1] In that year the Duke Borcziwoi was visiting the king of the neighbouring state of Moravia, when he was brought to the knowledge of the gospel through the agency of Methodius, a Christian priest, who accompanied him on his return to his country.

The Duchess Ludomilla and a number of the most distinguished Bohemians became converts; but the establishment of Christianity was not to be a tranquil one. The jealousy of the heathen population brought about a civil war, in which the newly converted duke was driven into exile. He was subsequently recalled, but compelled to abdicate in favour of his son Wratislav, who was married to Drahomira, or Dragomira, a princess, who was one of the staunchest supporters of the old heathen creed.

At Wratislav's death, Dragomira took the reins of government into her own hands, and set on foot severest measures for the suppression of Christianity. The Christians, driven to extremity, took up arms, and a struggle followed in which they were victorious; but the heathen princess, enraged at her defeat, contrived to have her pious mother-in-law, the Duchess Ludomilla,

---

[1] See Introductory Chapter.

c 2

assassinated while at prayer in her own private chapel. The name of this Christian princess is the first which stands on the long and glorious muster-roll of martyrs to which Bohemia can lay claim. The struggle ended with the government remaining in the hands of the elder of Drahomira's two sons, Wenzel, also called Wenzeslav. This prince had been educated by his grandmother Ludomilla, and was an earnest and determined upholder of the gospel.' He seems to have acted with forbearance and generosity to the defeated: but his mother's bitter hatred to Christianity made her the implacable enemy of her own son. She dared not attack him openly, and therefore had recourse to stratagem.

Her younger son, Bolislav,[1] was entirely in her interest, and, though a nominal Christian, was willing to be the tool of his wicked mother. He was about to celebrate the christening of his infant child, and invited his brother Wenzel to the ceremony.

The young duke arrived, and was received with much show of kindness by his mother and brother; a magnificent banquet was served, and the guests separated late.

Suspicious of some sinister design, Wenzel would not retire to his chamber, but passed into the church, intending to spend the night in prayer. If he thought the sanctity of the place would preserve him, he was mistaken; his treacherous brother, stirred up by their mother, found him kneeling at the altar, and stabbed him then and there in cold blood in 936.

This murder was followed up by a bitter persecution of the Christians, which lasted till the death of

---

[1] Afterwards called Bolislav the Cruel. See Introductory Chapter.

Drahomira, who, according to a legend, was swallowed up by an earthquake.

The Emperor Otho at last interfered, and by force of arms put a stop to the tyranny of Bolislav; he also insisted on the duke's children being placed under Christian instruction. Ultimately, when one of them, Bolislav the Pious, became reigning duke in 967, Christianity was definitely and finally established, and heathenism gradually died out.[1]

But almost as soon as the conquest with paganism had ended, a new struggle began. The enemy, wounded apparently to death, had risen up in a new form, and Bohemia was now about to enter on that terrible struggle with Rome which was to last for many centuries.

When the Bishop of Rome first claimed spiritual sovereignty over Christendom, about the eleventh century, resistance was made in Bohemia to the compulsory celibacy of the clergy and the denial of the cup to the laity. The pope endeavoured to force on the people the rites, ceremonial, and language of the Romish Church. This last imposition was especially obnoxious to the Bohemians, attached as they were to the use of their own tongue. A deputation was consequently sent to Rome to remonstrate against the new regulations, and to request that religious worship might still be conducted in the mother tongue. The request was granted, and the use of a litany in their own language permitted. This still exists.

But the license having been withdrawn at a later period, Duke Wratislaw—afterwards crowned king for his services to the empire—demanded through his ambassadors in Rome the re-establishment of the

See Introductory Chapter.

privilege. The answer he received from Gregory was as follows :—

" Bishop Gregory, servant of the servants of God, to Wratislaw, Duke of Bohemia, salutation and apostolic blessing. Among other requests that your highness has made us is, that we should restore, according to ancient practice, the celebration of the service in the Bohemian tongue. Know thou, beloved son, that we can in nowise consent to your request. We have, by careful searching of the Scriptures, come to the conviction that it has been and is pleasing to the Almighty to carry on His worship in a language which shall not be understood by all, at least not by the unlearned. For if it is sung openly by all together, it may easily be despised and thought little of ; or if it be misunderstood by some imperfectly taught, errors may slip in which it may be difficult to eradicate from the hearts of men. It is true that in the earlier times of the Church, indulgence was shown to a simple and ignorant people ; but since experience shows us that evils and even heresies have grown out of this indulgence, it has been decided that Christian order will not permit of its being any longer allowed. What your people demand cannot therefore be granted, and we forbid it by the authority of God and St. Peter, and command you to suppress this folly as much as possible."

The Bohemians did not submit to this spiritual tyranny without a struggle. When Pope Celestine endeavoured, in 1197, to enforce the celibacy of the clergy in Prague, through his legate, Cardinal Peter of Lataira, the unwelcome ambassador narrowly escaped stoning. It was not till 1350 that the celebration of the communion in one kind could be enforced.

About this time two remarkable men began to attract public attention in Prague—John Milicz, a canon of the cathedral, and his colleague Conrad Steckna. Milicz,[1] a man of high family and ardent spirit, was, on account of his rare attainments and purity of life, chosen as the preacher at the cathedral church in the citadel. He urged the people to frequent communion, in both kinds, and declaimed with power against the abuses in the Church. He left behind him writings in which he declares that he went to Rome with a strong impression on his mind that the great Antichrist was already come and reigning. He had prayed to God with fasting and supplications that, if this impression was not from above, the Lord would free him from it. But he found no rest for his soul. His impression was strengthened by what he saw. Leaving Rome, he wrote to some of the cardinals, declaring that the Antichrist was come and actually "sitting in the Church of God."

He defended this view in several discussions. At last he and his adherents were condemned by a bull of Gregory XI., and he was given up to the archbishop, who threw him into prison, from which he was only released in 1366, from fear of a popular rising in his favour. He persisted in maintaining his views, and died quietly eight years later.

Of Steckna we know less than of his companion. But Milicz's mantle appears to have fallen on his successor, Matthias Janov of Prague, commonly called "Parisius," because he had studied for nine years in Paris. He was confessor to Charles IV., Emperor of Germany, even before he had been invested with the imperial

[1] See Note A, Appendix.

dignity. He maintained the right of the laity to the cup in the Lord's Supper with even more zeal and force than his predecessor.[1]

When Charles IV. became emperor, Janov is said to have waited on him with a deputation of his colleagues, to ask for a general convocation for the reformation of the Church. The emperor replied he had no power to grant this, but would apply to his Holiness the Pope, to whose province it belonged.

The emperor did write, accordingly; but the pope was extremely indignant, and insisted on the punishment of the heretics. The emperor's fears prevailed, at last, over his affection for Janov, and he banished him the country.

Janov, however, subsequently returned; but spent the rest of his life in retirement. On his death-bed he comforted his friends with these words :

" The wrath of the enemies of the truth has prevailed, but only for a time. An humble and despised people shall be raised up, without arms or earthly force, which man shall not be able to overcome."

These words were truly prophetic. Meanwhile, witnesses to the truth were never wholly wanting. Many met in secret to receive the communion in both kinds, which was now strictly forbidden. These meetings were frequented at peril of life. On their way to them many were seized, beaten, robbed, and even drowned in the rivers. The communicants were at last driven to go armed and in large numbers. This state of things continued for many years.

But a greater witness to the truth was to appear, and combat the enemy with arms not of this world. Two

---

[1] See Note B, Appendix.

years before Janov's death, which occurred in 1394, the famous Bethlehem Church was founded. Its first preacher died in 1400, six years after Janov's decease, and was succeeded by John Huss.

This remarkable man, as is well known, began with denouncing the pride, luxury, and profligacy of the nobles and rich citizens. As long as these denunciations were directed only to the laity, he was looked on as an inspired oracle; but when he turned his attention to the clergy, and attacked their vices with the same plainness and boldness of speech, he was accused by them, like his Master before him, of being "possessed with a devil."

Some of the magnates were the first to bring complaints against Huss before the king; but Wolfrain, Archbishop of Prague, stood up in Huss's defence, declaring that he had been pledged at his ordination not to respect persons, but to preach the truth boldly. When he attacked the clergy, Wolfrain was the first to echo the complaints he had silenced before. The king, however, retorted by referring to the prelate's own words—that Huss was pledged to speak without espect of persons. Thus the courageous preacher escaped for the time.

But in the very year (1400) in which he became preacher of the Bethlehem chapel, Jerome of Prague returned from a visit to England, bringing with him the works of Wycliffe, which he circulated widely. Huss was among those who read them. The good seed had fallen into prepared ground; and from that time Huss appears to have made material progress in the clearness of his views of gospel truth.

Four years later, two English students, Jacob and

Conrad of Canterbury, came to Prague, and matriculated in that university. They were disciples of the English reformer, and spoke boldly of the abuses of the Romish Church, till they were silenced by a public prohibition. But, though silenced, they were not disheartened; for they had recourse to another mode of teaching. With their landlord's sanction, they had a picture painted in the dining-room of their lodging-house, depicting on one side the sufferings of Christ, and on the other the splendour of the Papal court. This picture seems first to have roused John Huss to the conviction of the contrast between the character of Christ and His teaching on the one hand, and His so-called "Vicar" on the other. Many were drawn to the house to see for themselves this silent witness to the truth.

In 1408 Wycliffe's works were formally examined and condemned, and their reading forbidden, under pain of banishment, by a council of forty magistrates and a number of the university doctors. Huss appears to have ascribed this decision to the preponderance of German influence; and seeing that the Germans were assuming the chief power in the university of Prague, he publicly proposed that the majority of votes which should decide a question should be reckoned among the Bohemians alone, and not include Germans or other foreigners. Much indignation was excited among the Germans by this proposal. King Wenzel was appealed to; and at the expiration of a year he decided in favour of the Bohemians. The Germans, offended, left the university for those of neighbouring countries; and this led to the foundation of the colleges of Erfurt and Leipzig. The Bohemians chose John Huss as the rector of the university.

The monks, alarmed at these steps, worked on the Archbishop von Hasenberg, an ignorant man, to condemn again, and even more publicly, the works of Wycliffe. Æneas Sylvius affirms that two hundred copies were given to the flames, all beautifully written and bound in costly covers with gold clasps.

In the year 1411, Pope John XXIII. proclaimed a war against the King of Naples, and issued an indulgence for all who should engage in it. One of the sellers of the indulgence came to Prague, and exhorted all men to come to this war as to a crusade. Such indignation was excited by the proclamation and the indulgence that in three churches preachers came forward to declare that the Pope of Rome must be Antichrist, because he urged Christians to make war on one another. These three preachers—one of very humble station—were seized, thrown into prison, and, in spite of the intercession of the university and even of the common people, were dragged before the judges, condemned, and executed.

These proceedings aroused a vehement outburst of feeling. A party of students took possession of the corpses, and carried them to their burial with solemn chants and expressions of sympathy.

The plot was now thickening. Huss lectured publicly in the church, Jerome in the university, on a series of theses against the indulgences. The lectures were numerously attended; and the public sympathy, in spite of opposition from those in power, grew and deepened.

In 1413 Huss was summoned to Rome; and as he did not obey the summons, the pope visited his disobedience on Prague, by laying it under an interdict. Seeing that his presence increased the spirit of dissension, the brave reformer voluntarily left Prague. From

town to town he proceeded, preaching the Word of God
faithfully and boldly, till the time came when he was to
be summoned to the Council of Constance, under the
emperor's safe-conduct, to defend his opinions.   With
a resolute though sorrowing heart he took a last leave
of his friends and his beloved country, and set out to
meet his doom.   He suffered death at the stake, as is
well known, in direct violation of his safe-conduct, on
July 6, 1415.[1]   His friend Jerome of Prague was also
burned, on the 30th of May in the following year.

Thus the work of reformation in Bohemia was
sealed by the blood of two of her best and noblest
defenders.   But the rage of their enemies was not
satiated.   The struggle was now a twofold one ; both
religious liberty and Bohemian nationality were at stake,
and the object of the adherents of the papacy was to
crush both.   But this was no easy task.   The tide of
popular feeling was strong.   Fifty-eight of the most
distinguished nobles of Bohemia drew up a paper, which
they signed and sent to the council, bitterly complaining of the unjust condemnation of their blameless and
faithful pastor, Huss.   The Moravian nobility did the
same.   But neither body of remonstrants received any
answer.   On the contrary, certain priests who had taken
an active part on the papal side were requested by the
fathers of the council to take the direction of the
affairs of the Church for the suppression of heresy.

And now a bitter strife began between the partisans
of Rome and the "Hussite" party, as it was called.
This party included many whose patriotism and desire
for liberty was a far stronger principle than any zeal for
religion.   From this time, in fact, the struggle was a

---

[1] See Introductory Chapter.

national one. A violent popular insurrection took place in July, 1419, in Prague, and the mob actually seized and massacred some of the town-council.

Martin v. had meanwhile been elected pope by the council. He began with conciliatory exhortations to the Hussites ; but he afterwards changed his soft words for threats, and fulminated excommunications against them, exhorting all the States of Germany to rise up and crush the movement, and promising forgiveness of sins to the worst criminal who killed a single Bohemian. This appeal eventually led to the famous Hussite war.

In the meantime Sigismund, at the death of Wenzel, had assumed the government of Bohemia, and taken active measures to suppress heresy.

The Hussites had begun to divide themselves into two parties. The larger and more moderate of these comprised those who were chiefly anxious to restore the communion in both kinds, who were thence denominated *Calixtines* or *Utraquists.*[1] These men were generally for peaceful measures, and willing to agree to some compromise with the papal party.

The more zealous and determined partisans gathered together in a position of defence, and many of them took refuge on a rocky height about ten miles from Prague. They gave this hill the name of "Tabor," surrounded it with a wall, and built a fortified town, which they were prepared to defend by force of arms. The members of this party were hence called "Tabor-ites," and were regarded with hostility and dread by Calixtines as well as papists.[2]

---

[1] The device on their standard was a chalice, in token of their desire that the cup should be granted to the laity, which they seem to have regarded as the main point at issue.

[2] See Introductory Chapter.

The Taborites, however, made overtures of peace, and sent deputies to the city of Kuntenberg. But the people of the town were chiefly on the papal side. They seized the deputies, and threw them over the precipices near their town. Fresh deputations were sent, and all treated in the same manner. The "Martyrs of Kuntenberg," as they were called, were commemorated, and sermons were preached on the anniversary of their death, even down to the middle of the seventeenth century.

But many besides the Taborite ambassadors were now to seal their faith with their blood. A few instances may suffice.

John Krasa, a leading merchant of Prague, spoke plainly, during a journey of business he made in Silesia, against Huss's condemnation, and in favour of the right of all to partake of the cup in the Lord's Supper. He was overheard, seized, and thrown into prison.

The next day, Nicolas of Bethlehem, a student of Prague, who had been sent to Breslau to plead this same right, was put into the same prison. The young confessor was received by his fellow-captive with a warm welcome. "My brother Nicolas," he said, "how great is the honour to which we are called, that we should be witnesses for our Lord Jesus! Let us joyfully submit to this light affliction—the conflict is short, the recompense eternal. Let us remember Him who, to shed His precious blood to redeem us, suffered so cruel a death for us; and remember, too, what others have borne for His sake."

Thus did Krasa encourage and exhort his young companion. But, alas! the courage of poor Nicolas failed when he was led to the place of execution and saw the terrible preparations. The pope's legate, who stood by, profited by the weakness of the poor young man, and working on his hopes of escape, induced him to recant his " Hussite errors."

His companion stood firm as a rock. Entreaties and threats had no effect. He was tied by the feet to a horse, and dragged through the streets. The legate followed him, entreating him to "have pity on himself and recant." But Krasa only replied, "I am ready to die for the gospel of the Lord Jesus." Bruised, wounded, and half dead, he was brought to the place of execution, and there burned at the stake.

Soon after, twenty-four of the principal citizens of the town of Leitmeritz were arrested on a similar charge, and imprisoned in the fortress by order of the burgomaster, a hard-hearted and cruel man, and a bigoted adherent of the papacy. They remained long in prison, and at last, half dead with hunger and cold, were laid bound on carts and dragged to the banks of the Elbe to be drowned. The people were greatly moved. The friends and families of the prisoners crowded round with loud lamentations and entreaties.

Among the condemned was the husband of the burgomaster's daughter. The heart-broken wife fell at her father's feet and implored him, in an agony of grief, to spare her husband's life. "Stop your weeping!" cried the hard-hearted father. "You know not what you ask. Cannot you find a worthier husband?" The young wife rose from her knees. "You shall never again give me in marriage, my father," she said, resolutely; and with weeping and lamentation she followed in the melancholy train that accompanied the victims to the place of their death.

The martyrs were taken from their carts and placed in boats. During the preparations they all raised their voices and called on heaven and earth to witness their innocence. They then took a last leave of their families and friends, exhorting them to firmness and zeal, and especially reminding them to trust more to the word of God than to the commands of men. They then prayed for their enemies, and devoutly commending their souls to God, they were carried in the boats into the middle of the stream, and, bound hand and foot, were flung into the river. The executioners stood on the shore with pikes, to prevent the possibility of any, in their dying struggles, reaching the shore.

But they could not separate the devoted wife from her husband. She sprang into the river, and throwing her arms round him, made a vain effort to rescue him from the waves, nerved by a love stronger than death. It was vain; the water was too deep; the faithful pair sank together: and their corpses were found next day, still locked in each other's embrace. Death had failed to part them; they were united for eternity.

These were not the only martyrs for the truth at this terrible time. The pastor Wenzel of Arnestowitz, a blameless and pious man, was condemned, with his assistant, for having administered the communion in both kinds. Three peasants and four boys were to share his fate, for having received the cup from him.

"Either I am right, or you must cancel the Scriptures," said the pastor, boldly. To the last they made every effort to induce him to recant; but he replied he would rather die a hundred deaths than deny the truth as clearly written in the Gospels. He seated himself calmly on the scaffold, taking his brave young companions on his knees, and surrounded by his other fellow-victims; and all of them died firmly in the flames.

Several others followed. Many were put to deaths too horrible to recount, but all seem to have shown the true spirit of Christian martyrs. "Pray for yourselves," said one, as he was led to the place of execution, "and for those who lead you astray, that God may in His mercy bring you out of darkness into light."

CHAPTER II.

THE two parties of Calixtines and Taborites were now becoming more and more sharply defined. The Calixtines were desirous of retaining as much as possible of the Romish rites and ceremonies. Even those among them who were most sincere and upright were not exempt from this bias; but, unhappily, this was not all. Secret emissaries of the pope and emperor had joined their ranks, and laboured to promote division and mutual hatred, and to stir up the people against the advocates of pure gospel truth, whom they designated by the hated name of "Picards," the name which had already been given in derision to the Waldenses.

Thus the excitement and tumult on both sides increased daily. John of Selau, a monk and parish priest of a church in the new town of Prague, a man of great eloquence and fervour, preached to large congregations in favour of the pure gospel doctrines. He became obnoxious to the Romish party, who, on pretext of convoking a secret council, enticed the preacher and twelve of his followers into the town-hall, and there hastily condemned and beheaded them. Their fate was discovered to the people by the blood which streamed from under the closed doors. A crowd pressed up to the town-hall, broke open the doors, and sought for the bodies. The head of Selau was borne through the town by a priest named Gaudentius, who called on all to take vengeance for the deed. Some of the councillors were beaten and others put to flight by the mob; the corpses of the victims were displayed in the church, and solemnly carried to their burial.

The preacher, when he rose to speak, could hardly command his voice when he heard the loud weeping and sobbing around him, and saw some borne out fainting from the church. Repressing his emotion, he gave out for his text Acts viii. 2, "And devout men carried Stephen to his burial, and made great lamentation over him." At the end of the sermon he lifted up the bleeding head of the victim, and with tears and earnest words entreated his hearers to keep in mind all they had heard from their faithful pastor, and not to allow even an angel from heaven to teach them otherwise.

The spirit of division, as might be expected, grew fiercer. In 1427 Przibran and Prokop, the two "administrators" of the council, with two other distinguished men, were seized and banished for their adherence to gospel teaching, by the Calixtines.

It would have been no wonder had so divided a party been annihilated by the papal adherents; but, happily, through the overruling mercy of God, the appearance of an imperial army, sent by Sigismund in compliance with the pope's desire, before mentioned, alarmed the Hussites into union. For a time all strife was forgotten, and all agreed to place Prokop and John Ziska at the head of affairs.[1] This extraordinary man, who,

---

[1] John Ziska, or "the One-eyed," as is well known, lost his only remaining eye in battle, but continued his military operations with unabated zeal and a skill truly wonderful in one so disabled.

in spite of blindness, was the first general of his day, succeeded, by his dauntless resolution and consummate generalship, in defeating the Imperialists. Prague lay at his mercy, and the Hussite cause, for the time, gained the day. The emperor, foiled in the field, had recourse to other means.

In 1432 a council was called at Basle, to which the Bohemians were courteously invited, that they might be convinced of their errors by kindness. All personal security was promised them. After Huss's death such promises were little likely to inspire confidence; but John Rokycana of Prague and Nicolas Episcopius of Tabor went as representatives respectively of the Calixtine and Taborite parties.

Their reception was friendly. They requested the consent of the council to four principal articles, which were as follows:—

1. That the celebration of Divine service in their own tongue, and the administration of the cup to the laity, should be restored.

2. That the clergy should not mingle in political affairs.

3. That the Word of God should be freely taught.

4. That open vice in the clergy should be openly punished.

The legate asked, contemptuously, "Are these all your articles? You are said to believe that the monks came from the devil." "Where else should they come from," replied Prokop, "when they have never been founded either by patriarchs or prophets, or by Christ and His apostles?"

In spite of this bold rejoinder the outward harmony of the meeting was not overthrown. A debate was held for fifty days between disputants chosen on each side, but with no result. The enemies of the faith were now to try persuasion, and one of the deputies was unhappily an easy prey.

Rokycana, the deputy of the Calixtine party, though he had been a talented and eloquent preacher of gospel truth, lacked the "single eye" which is needed for its champion. He was worldly and ambitious, and, dazzled by the prospect of being made Archbishop of Prague, easily consented to yield the point at issue. "None can tempt like the fallen;" and he used arts of flattery and cajolery to induce his companions to yield.

He was only too successful. The four articles were granted on condition of their promising complete obedience to Rome. The other representatives fell into the snare; and the council and the emperor sent ambassadors to Bohemia to announce that the people of that country were now received as faithful children into the bosom of the Church.

The Bohemian senate met on this occasion, and Rokycana pointed out to them that they had now received a solemn promise in confirmation of the rights for which so much blood had been shed. He urged them to be satisfied, in language very different from that he had formerly employed, when he had spoken of the pope and the emperor as the Woman of Babylon and the Beast of the Apocalypse. Many of his hearers were uneasy at the spirit of compromise he now showed. The Taborites especially were displeased. They had again recourse to arms; but this time they had not Ziska for their leader: they were totally defeated, and their military force entirely crushed, in the year 1434.

The following year Rokycana was chosen archbishop

by the senate.   The emperor, who appears to have distrusted him, refused to confirm the decision, and Rokycana was fain to fly from Prague and remain for three years at a distance.

Soon after this Sigismund died.   His successor, Albert, only survived two years, leaving a son, who was brought up at the imperial court.

George Podiebrad took the regency during this interregnum.   He was entirely under the influence of Rokycana.   The pope was furious against Podiebrad and the Calixtines, who in their turn inveighed against the pope and the monastic orders; while both parties agreed in oppressing those who followed the pure gospel teaching.

Rokycana now began to play a double game with the remnant of the conquered Taborites.   He declared he would willingly embrace their tenets if they could prove their truth, and proposed an open discussion before the senate on their points of difference.   The Taborites fell into the snare, and appeared before the council with full confidence in their righteous cause.   Umpires were chosen, and it was declared that on whichever side the decision should be made, the opposite party should be held bound to give in its adhesion.

But the whole affair had been privately arranged to give the advantage to the Calixtines.   The decision was given in their favour, and the Taborites perceived they had been victims to a stratagem.   They dared not refuse the conditions.   On returning to their own city they endeavoured to obtain some days' respite, but Podiebrad had the city surrounded with an army, and they were at last forced or alarmed into a surrender. The Taborite clergy were seized and imprisoned, and most of them recanted altogether; a few only went over to the Calixtines.

In the meantime the election of Rokycana as archbishop was not ratified by the pope. Many efforts were made to obtain his consent; but he would only give it on condition of Rokycana yielding the point at issue as to the administration of the Lord's Supper.

In 1448 Cardinal St. Angelo came to Prague, with the view of wresting from the Bohemians the articles which had been granted them, and which were entitled "The Compact." Rokycana now changed his tone—he was again loud in his invectives against the pope, called him the great Antichrist of the Scriptures, and used such strong language in favour of reform that many thought a new Huss had arisen.

Alas! they were mere words. He was not one prepared to act as well as speak. He had, however, a near relative very different from himself—Gregory of Raserherz, his sister's son, a man of noble birth, and one to whom his religion was indeed a reality.

Gregory and some of his friends were so deeply impressed with Rokycana's sermons that they came to him to open their minds to him and seek for his counsel. He received them with the utmost cordiality, praised their zeal, recommended the study of certain writings on the divisions of the Church, and spoke altogether in a manner to increase their ardour. At the same time he advised, for the present, silence and patience.

Meanwhile he endeavoured to form an alliance with the Greek Church, in hopes of obtaining support against the pope. His overtures were met in a friendly spirit, but there was little hope of any really efficient aid.

Rokycana, however, made the most of it, and declared the Reformation was at hand. "We are only working on the surface," he said; "soon those will appear who will dig deep and firmly fix the foundation of the truth."

For seven years he continued to soothe the true reformers with these fair words; and when further pressed, always replied that "he was giving the matter consideration, and that he knew not what to advise, there were so many difficulties on all sides."

His hearers, more in earnest than himself, declared they were ready to follow him, and acknowledge him as their guide, teacher, and spiritual father. But he was not prepared to take so dangerous a part. He put them off with vain excuses. "You are appointing me," he said, "to a charge too onerous for me. The cause is fraught with peril; you are too bold: we must wait."

Meanwhile it had been plainly shown how little the Greek Church could be looked to for help. Constantinople had been taken by the Turks (in 1453); and two of the Greek refugees who came to Prague were cordially welcomed by Rokycana, and allowed to celebrate mass.

But it was soon apparent that a superstitious and vain ceremonial had completely destroyed the simplicity of their faith. This opened the eyes of Rokycana's pious hearers. They again went to him, and entreated him to have compassion on those souls led astray, and not to leave them in so perplexing a condition.

Rokycana might now have taken the place of Huss. But he had neither courage nor singleness of heart for such an undertaking. He was not prepared to bear the reproach of Christ. He proposed to his too eager disciples to go their own way, and let him go his. He would intercede with George Podiebrad (now made king) for a place of safety for them, in which they could live peaceably, and worship according to their conscience. This promise he kept. He succeeded in obtaining for them the district of Litiz, in the Silesian mountains. Here all who were anxious for a real reformation repaired in 1459. They assembled together, and occupied themselves with the study of the Scriptures and with good works, receiving teachers from those of the Calixtines who were willing to lay aside all superstitious practices and vain ceremonies, and return to apostolic simplicity.

This little band of Christians, bound together by such close ties, began to give each other the title of "Brethren," which they have retained to this day. And so the first foundation of the Bohemian Brethren's Church was laid.

CHAPTER III.

BUT this new Church was to meet with persecution in its very infancy. The priests were unwearied in seeking to stir up the people against the new community. "Quench the spark," they said, "before it becomes a flame." And, like their Master, the members of the infant Church were to be "wounded in the house of their friends." Rokycana himself—the first adviser and friend of the Brethren—was now to prove false to them. He had been trying to serve two masters; and the world, as always happens in such cases, had gained the victory. The consistency and zeal of the Brethren were a reproach to himself. He accused them of rashness and presumption; and pretexts were not wanting to bring them into bad odour with the king and council.

On one occasion, in the year 1461, Gregory, the nephew of Rokycana, who was one of the principal leaders in the little community at Litiz, was visiting some of his friends and disciples in Prague, where they were holding a meeting in a private house. They were discovered and betrayed;[1] and the judge—who was in his heart well disposed towards them, but dared not refuse to act in his official capacity—came to arrest

---

[1] It appears from other accounts that they were warned by one who was secretly their friend, and advised quickly to disappear; but that in their fiery zeal the majority determined to await their doom.

them, and, standing at the door of the room where they were assembled, pronounced these remarkable words: "All who live godly in Christ Jesus must suffer persecution. You who are assembled here, follow me to prison."

The king's mind had been poisoned against the Brethren by false accusers, who alleged that they were about to organize an insurrection like that of the Taborites. On this suspicion the little band had been arrested; and the pious Gregory was stretched on the rack, with a view of drawing some confession from him.

But He who has promised to be with His people in the furnace was with His faithful servant in this extremity. Gregory fell into a kind of trance, in which he lay insensible to pain, and apparently dead. The torturers desisted from their work, thinking it too late; and Rokycana was informed that his nephew had expired on the rack. He hastened to the spot, and when he saw his brave and devoted relative lying pale and deathlike before him, his conscience was awakened: he wept over him in bitter agony of spirit, exclaiming again and again, "O my Gregory, would I were where thou art!"

Gregory, on recovering consciousness after some hours, related a kind of dream or vision he had had during his apparent swoon. He thought he had been led into a meadow of wondrous beauty, in the midst of which stood a tree laden with fruit, of which birds of many kinds in the branches were partaking. A youth stood by, who ruled these birds with a wand, and permitted none to fly from their places. Three men seemed to guard the tree, of whose countenances he took special note. This dream was afterwards considered prophetic.

At Rokycana's request Gregory was set free; but the time-serving man was not willing to render any further help to the infant Church. All religious services, if held without the Romish ceremonies, were strictly forbidden; and anyone who took the office of minister among the "Picards" was liable to be punished with death.

In vain the persecuted band entreated Rokycana to come to their aid, and not to abandon a cause which he well knew was that of God. He was deaf to all their representations; and at last they took leave of him in a letter containing these words: "Thou art of the world, and wilt perish with the world." Stung by a reproach of which he must have felt the justice, he revenged himself by stirring up the king to a fresh persecution of the Brethren.

Most of the members of the little band were scattered, and their principal leaders driven to hide in caves and woods, and even there were in fear of their lives. Only by night did they venture to kindle a fire, lest the smoke should betray them. In the bitter cold of a Bohemian winter evening in the mountains, they gathered round these camp-fires, reading the Scriptures by their light, and edifying one another by spiritual converse. When they met together in the snow, they were careful to tread singly in each other's footsteps, while the last comer effaced the tracks with a snow-covered pine-twig, so as to make them appear as if a peasant had been drawing a faggot after him. From their life in caves and holes of the earth, they were called by their adversaries in derision "Jamnici," or

" Pitmen." It was a title of which they had no reason
to be ashamed.

In the midst of these dangers the Brethren set themselves earnestly to the work of organizing their Church,
and setting apart certain persons for the ministerial
office. It was a solemn undertaking, carried on with
frequent meetings for deliberation and much prayer.
Finding that they could not look for help from those
who had been in Romish orders, they resolved to exercise
the right which they believed Christ had given to His
disciples, by choosing from among themselves men fitted
for the sacred office.

After long prayer and consultation, they met at a
village called Sbota to choose their principal leaders.
Nine men were fixed on, and a child was called in to
draw lots. There were three slips with the word " Est "
on them. These three fell to the lot of the three men
whom Gregory had seen in his dream.

These three men—who seem to have been in different
ways well fitted for the ministering office—were sent
into Austria to receive consecration from the hands of
Stephanus, the ·bishop of a community of Waldenses
who had been driven from the south of France or Pied-
mont, and had emigrated to Austria.

Stephanus consecrated the three men bishops; and
there was some thought of uniting the new Church
with this community of Austrian Waldenses. The
Bohemian Brethren objected that the Waldenses had
fallen insensibly into a spirit of compromise, and were
in the habit of frequenting the Romish ceremonies to
avoid persecution. They represented this to the
Austrian Waldenses, who appear to have received the
brotherly admonition in the same Christian spirit in

which it was offered, and freely owned that they had fallen away from the purity of their fathers' practice, and must seek to return to their former high standard.

A time and place were fixed for a meeting to decide on the union of the Bohemians and Waldenses. But the intended meeting was heard of, and made the pretext for a fresh persecution of the Austrian Waldenses. Stephanus was burned in Vienna, and his flock compelled to fly. The greater number took refuge in Brandenburg, which was afterwards a gathering-place for the Moravians.

The persecution of these Austrian Waldenses was quickly followed by one no less severe of the Bohemian Brethren. King George Podiebrad issued an edict commanding that every nobleman should seek out and apprehend all the " Picards " he could find on his estate, and force or alarm them into conformity to the dominant church. Many were arrested and imprisoned in this manner.

In 1471 Rokycana's career was terminated by death. He might well have desired to exchange his death-bed for his pious nephew's couch in the torture-chamber. He died in all the agonies of utter despair.

The king visited him in his dying hour. We have no details of the last awful interview between the persecuting monarch and the teacher who had been his tempter to evil : all we hear is, that Rokycana solemnly summoned his royal pupil to meet him at the judgment-seat of God.

And whether this summons acted on the king's mind so as to verify itself, or that it was one of those cases in which the dying seem gifted with prevision, it is certain that Podiebrad only survived Rokycana a month. He was succeeded by Wladislas of Poland—himself a mild and merciful prince, but led into acts of severity by his advisers, and especially by his bigoted wife.

Accusations were brought on all sides against the Brethren, and their position was rendered more painful by internal dissensions. A discussion had arisen among them as to the lawfulness of holding offices of state, entering the army, &c. The majority had no scruples on these heads; but a small minority held the views afterwards called Mennonite,[1] and formed a community by themselves at Prague. In itself such a discussion need have been of little moment; but, unhappily, the apostle's precepts of mutual forbearance were forgotten, and the minority who had separated accused their brethren of worldliness of views—an accusation which was easily exaggerated into an intention to resort to arms to strengthen their claims.

At this time the Brethren were summoned to appear before the council and give an account of their opinions. It was a matter of anxious deliberation with them whether or not they should comply with this summons. They had too much reason to suspect a snare; but they decided that the risk of being entrapped must be run, and two representatives were chosen and sent forth, feeling that they would probably meet the fate of Huss.

A letter, written by Baron Rostha, one of their principal leaders, to one of the deputies, shows the spirit which animated them.

"It is a part of our human nature," he writes, "to cling to life. But thou, my brother, hast been better taught. Thou mayest remember that thy life is buried with Christ, and to win it thou must have died with Him.

---

[1] The sect of Mennonites exists in Germany to this day.

Thou knowest in whom thou hast trusted, and with whose power thou wilt keep a good conscience to the end. Be strong then in the Lord, and in the power of His might, and fight the good fight unto the end, and thou shalt receive the crown of life. I will not hold thee back, beloved brother; stand fast, and fear not. What human foresight could do to secure the safety of you both we have done, and will do; but if the wrath of the enemy should be too strong, and it should be the will of the Lord that His cause should be glorified by your death, be ready to say with Job, 'The Lord gave, and the Lord taketh away; blessed be the name of the Lord.'"

But it was God's will to deliver His servants on this occasion. On the very day of the council meeting, the chief magistrate, who was one of the Brethren's bitterest enemies, died suddenly; other hindrances supervened, and the council was indefinitely put off, and the deputies dismissed in safety.

The queen now urged her husband Wladislas to a fresh edict against the Brethren. He yielded, against his own convictions, but was so deeply distressed at what he had done, that he retired to his room and fell on his knees, and implored God that the guilt of the bloody edict might not be imputed to him, and that its consequences might if possible, be averted.

The prayer was answered in a manner little expected by the kind-hearted but weak monarch. The queen was suddenly taken ill, and died, leaving a new-born infant, who afterwards came to the throne under the name of Ludwig.

This gave a respite to the Brethren; but two years later some of the bishops most hostile to them per-

suaded the king to press the edict. The pastors of the
Church were obliged to fly or conceal themselves; and
several of the people were arrested. Among others, six
men of humble station, artisans and peasants, were
brought before Baron von Schwanberg, in the town of
Huiden. The priest asked them if they would follow
him as their spiritual shepherd. "The Shepherd of
our souls is Jesus Christ," they replied. They were led
to execution. But the captain of the guard, who had a
friendly feeling for Nicolas, the youngest of the six,
proposed to get him a year's respite for consideration.
Nicolas paused a moment, but quickly exclaimed, "It
would be abandoning my brethren even to allow myself
to deliberate. I will die with them." He mounted the
scaffold with his companions, and all died firmly and
joyfully in the flames.

The Calixtines themselves did not escape persecution.
Those who preached scriptural and pure doctrine were
banished, imprisoned, and several put to the torture;
one actually died on the rack.

The archbishopric of Prague was at this time vacant,
and the Calixtines during the interregnum were only
permitted to have their priests ordained in Italy, and
that, generally speaking, by men devoted to the papacy.
Twice, however, they had Italian bishops, who showed
themselves friendly to the gospel; but eventually the
priests ordained by them were compelled to submit to
the pope. Some candidates for ordination were so much
disgusted that they actually went to receive the ordination rite in Armenia, which was given them there in consideration of their agreement on some particular points.

Meanwhile, Luther was beginning to rise into notice.
His example stirred up the zeal of many Calixtines for

E

pure gospel doctrine, and some were inclined to seek
ordination at Wittenburg rather than Rome. An
Assembly of the Bohemian and Moravian States was
convened in 1523, to which ecclesiastics of different
churches were invited, and twenty articles of reformation were drawn up under the superintendence of the
head of the university. The preacher, Gallus Cahera,
was chosen administrator. Cahera was a professed
friend and admirer of Luther ; and the advocates of the
Reformation thought they had gained a champion. They
were grievously deceived. Cahera was a traitor, who
had been all along secretly working for the papacy. He
contrived, by dint of intrigue, to have a fresh set of articles brought forward, favourable to the Romish Church.

The weak and vacillating though well-intentioned
King Wladislas was dead, and was succeeded by his son
Ludwig. The young king, a warm adherent of the
papacy, was ready to abet the traitor's endeavours ; and
Cahera compelled all priests and citizens, on pain of
banishment, to sign these new articles. The old accusation was revived, that the " Evangelicals " or " Picards "
were plotting against the Calixtines ; and three of the
former were put to the torture to force disclosures from
them ; but in vain.

The charge of Picardism was now made the pretext
for every kind of oppression. Anyone who had debts
he was unwilling to pay had only to accuse his creditor
of being a *Picard,* to get him banished from the town.
The most shameless calumnies were listened to ; and
many Picards were scourged, branded, and banished.

In 1526, an aged and learned man, named Nicolas,
was brought before the magistrates on the charge of
Picardism. He was asked his views on the sacrament

of the altar. "I hold," he said, "what the evangelists and St. Paul teach us to believe." "Do you believe," said his questioner, " that Christ's body and blood are really present in the Lord's Supper ?" "I believe," replied the old man, "that when a pious servant of God shows forth in the assembly of believers the grace and mercy we have received through Christ's death, by distributing the bread and wine, that these elements then constitute the supper of the Lord, and by faith we are partakers of the benefits of Christ's death."

Some further questions were asked of Nicolas on the intercession of saints, the mass, &c. ; and he, with his hostess Clara, an aged widow, who held the same faith, was condemned to death by fire.

At the place of execution they were directed to adore the crucifix, which was placed towards the east ; but they replied, " The commandment of God forbids our worshipping the likeness of anything in heaven or earth. We will pray to the living God, Lord of heaven and earth, who dwells equally in the east and west, north and south."

And, turning from the crucifix, the two aged Christians raised their hands and eyes to heaven and prayed to Christ with fervour. They took leave of their respective children, and Nicolas, mounting the scaffold, repeated the Belief, commended his soul in solemn prayer to his Saviour, and afterwards repeated in Latin the psalm, "In Thee, O Lord, have I put my trust." His fellow-sufferer, Clara, was led to the scaffold beside him, and the pile was lighted which consumed these faithful witnesses to the truth.

Their death was followed, the next year, by that of Martha von Porzicz, a woman of heroic courage and constancy. When brought before the council, she boldly confessed her faith, and reproached the Calixtines for their cowardly flattery of the pope. The magistrate told her she must prepare the garments in which she was to suffer. "My dress and mantle are all ready," she quietly replied; "let me go as soon as you please."

The town-crier proclaimed before her that she was condemned for throwing contempt on the sacrament. "That is not true," she replied. "I am condemned because I will not blaspheme God by declaring that the actual body—flesh, bones, and blood—of Christ can be present in the sacrament. Do not believe these priests," she continued, addressing the people; "they are hypocrites, living for their own pleasure, and given up to vice."

On arriving at the place of execution, her persecutors pressed her to adore the crucifix, as they had done Nicolas and Clara. She turned away, and raising her eyes to heaven, exclaimed: "*There* is our God; to Him only must we look!" With these words she mounted the scaffold, and met her doom with serene composure.

Equal constancy was shown, the next year, by two brothers, workmen, condemned to suffer death by burning at Prague. On their way to execution they encouraged each other with words of Scripture. "As the Lord Jesus," said one of them, "has suffered such cruel pain for us, we will also endure this death, rejoicing that we are counted worthy to suffer for the Word of God." "Truly," replied his brother, "I never felt such joy, even on my wedding-day, as now."

When the fire was kindled, they both said in a clear

voice, " Lord Jesus Christ, Thou hast prayed for Thine
enemies on the cross ; we now pray Thee also, forgive
the king, the citizens, and the priests, for they know
not what they do, and their hands are defiled with
blood. Dear people," added one of them, turning to
the multitude, "pray for your king, that God may
give him the knowledge of the truth, for the priests are
deceiving him."   With these words the pious brothers
calmly met their fate, and expired in the flames.

The traitorous persecutor of the Picards, Cahera,
did not long prosper; the political intrigues into which
his restless spirit led him brought him into disgrace
with the king; he was banished, and ended his life in
France in great misery.

His removal did not, however, bring any relief to
the suffering Bohemian Church.   Under Ferdinand I.,
brother of Charles V., who now succeeded to the throne,
they had much oppression to suffer.   They were exposed
to lawless violence : to kill a "Picard " was regarded as
no greater fault than to kill a dog.

In spite of all this the Church grew and multiplied,
and the faithful brethren, entering into correspondence
with Luther and other German reformers, found in them
Christian friends ever ready to uphold them by warm
sympathy and strengthening words.

They needed all such help, for days of even deeper trial
were at hand. The Emperor Charles V., wishing to carry
out the decisions of the Council of Trent, commenced a
war against the Protestant princes of Germany; and his
brother Ferdinand readily lent his aid, and called on
his subjects to second him.   This they were, however,
reluctant to do : when, therefore, the German Protestants had been defeated in 1547, Ferdinand entered

Prague with an army of German and Hungarian soldiers, took possession of the city as a conqueror, and banished, imprisoned, scourged, and deprived of their property many of the most distinguished citizens. Many went voluntarily into exile, to avoid further oppression. In such a time of trouble it may easily be supposed that the pure Church of the Brethren was exposed to peculiar attacks from the malice of its foes. Calumnies were again brought forward, and an edict was issued for the closing of all places of worship belonging to the Brethren.

In five domains, largely inhabited by the members of this Church, the king commanded that all who would not either join the Romanists or Calixtines should be banished. The lords of these estates he took care to arrest on other pretexts.

It was a time of sifting for the infant Church. Many, alas! were driven by terror into outward conformity with the dominant powers. The more steadfast, preferring exile to apostasy, agreed to emigrate in three distinct bodies to Poland. They travelled by different roads, to elude suspicion, and met at Posen. They were kindly received by the Poles, though these were mostly Romanists, and remained at Posen till the bishop of the place obtained an edict of banishment against them.

They were then obliged to pass into Lower Prussia, where Duke Albert of Brandenburg allowed them to remain. Here they were questioned by some Lutheran divines in Königsberg, and by them acknowledged as brethren in the faith. Certain cities were allotted to them as dwelling-places; and Paul Speratus, Bishop of Pomerania, who had known them before, when on his travels, showed them special kindness and sympathy.

But Ferdinand's rancour against the Evangelical Church was not satiated. He issued a third edict, commanding that all the ministers of the Brethren's Church in Bohemia should be arrested and imprisoned. The greater number avoided this by flight; some going to Moravia, which was still unmolested, and others to places so near that they could secretly visit their faithful adherents by night, and occasionally hold services in private houses.

In this manner most escaped; but three principal pastors fell into the enemy's hands. The chief of these was John Augusta, a former disciple and subsequently a correspondent of Luther. He was looked on as one of the most powerful defenders of evangelical doctrines; pains were therefore taken to employ a false friend to entrap him, on the pretext of seeking his advice, into a private interview, at which he was arrested; he was then brought to Prague, and tortured fearfully three several times, as well as his colleague Bibek, in the hope of forcing them to make some disclosures which might implicate others.

Several of the nobility who adhered to the Brethren's Church were exiled or imprisoned, like the pastors; some of them, like John Augusta, were put to the torture. The heroic John Prostiborsky bit his tongue when on the rack, lest he should be driven by pain to make admissions which might injure his brethren. This he afterwards declared in writing; and soon after he died in prison from the effects of his sufferings.

Ferdinand, determined to spare no pains for the re-establishment of Popery as the only religion of Bohemia, took further measures to bring about this object. He sent for the Jesuits, and endowed them with a wealthy

college. They, with their usual policy, devoted themselves to the education of youth, thus poisoning the
springs in their very source.

The cause of evangelical religion might well have
seemed lost in Bohemia; but God in His mercy was
about to grant a period of rest to the sorely-tried
Brethren's Church.

In 1562 Ferdinand was succeeded by his son Maximilian, a monarch of gentle and merciful disposition;
he refused to allow of any persecution for conscience'
sake; and the persecuted Church was again enabled to
take root downwards and bear fruit upwards. Maximilian
had himself been instructed during his father's lifetime
in Divine truth, and much influenced by his pious tutor,
Johann Pfander, a distinguished preacher, and a man of
learning as well as piety.

These qualities, however, exposed Pfander to the
hatred of the Popish party, and pains were taken to
prejudice the Emperor Ferdinand against him. One
day Ferdinand entered the preacher's room, where he
found him alone, and reproached him bitterly with
having led his son astray by his teaching. Pfander
answered mildly and respectfully; but the emperor was
so carried away with passion, that he seized the preacher
by the throat, and was just on the point of stabbing
him. He, however, recovered himself, and was contented with commanding his son to dismiss the tutor.

Maximilian, however, did not imbibe his father's
principles: he was accustomed to observe, that to endeavour to rule consciences by force was in fact an
effort to take heaven by storm.

Among those about him who were like-minded with
himself was the distinguished physician Crato, to whom

he always gave his full confidence. One day the emperor was taking a walk alone with Crato; the conversation turned on the divisions by which Christendom was torn, and the emperor asked his favourite which of the varied Christian sects seemed to him to approach the most nearly to apostolic simplicity. "I do not know any of whom it can be said more truly, sire," replied Crato, "than of the Brethren, who are also called *Picards.*" "I believe that myself," replied the emperor.

This remark encouraged the good physician to advise the Brethren to dedicate their new hymn-book, of which they were preparing a German edition, to the emperor. They followed his counsel: and the dedication is still extant, in which they express the hope that the emperor would, like David, Josiah, Constantine, and Theodosius, act as a nursing father to the Church. There is every reason to believe that the will to do so was not wanting in the case of Maximilian; but he was surrounded by those who were able to hinder his efforts for good.

An attempt was made by the enemies of the gospel, in the third year of Maximilian's reign, to have an edict published against the Brethren. The chancellor, Joachim of Neuhaus, came to Vienna, and succeeded by art and determination in inducing the emperor, against his own will, to sign the edict.

But the attempt was frustrated in a remarkable manner. The chancellor had just left Vienna, and was crossing the Danube, when a part of the bridge over which he was passing gave way, and he and his suite were precipitated into the stream. A few of his attendants reached the shore. A youth of noble birth, who was among them, endeavoured to uphold his master till a boat came to his assistance; but it was too late to save his life. The body of the chancellor was brought out of the water; but the chest which contained the persecuting edict remained at the bottom of the river, and could never be rescued. Thus the danger was averted for the time. The young nobleman who had tried to save Neuhaus became a convert to the Brethren's faith, and lived to an advanced age.

In 1575, Maximilian held a general Council of State, and declared his "Utraquist" subjects free to draw up a general confession of faith, which would be recognised by the State. The term Utraquist (or partaker of the communion in both kinds) was, properly speaking, another name for the Calixtines; but it was here applied to all the Protestant confessions—Picards, Lutherans, and Calvinists (of these last two there were now a considerable number in Bohemia).

The Jesuits and "Pseudo-Hussites" availed themselves of the minor differences of these Churches to throw obstacles in the way of any general compact; but, in spite of all their intrigues, a form was drawn up, which all the Protestant confessions could subscribe.

In 1576 the excellent Maximilian died, and was succeeded by his son Rudolf, who was like-minded with his father, and for the first six years of his reign maintained, like Maximilian, entire religious liberty.

In 1602, a fresh effort at persecution was made by the Jesuits, under whose influence Rudolf passed an edict confirming the decrees of Wladislaw against the Picards. But the numerous influential noblemen who were friends to the Brethren succeeded in preventing the decree from being put in force, except in closing for a time some of their churches.

It was, indeed, quite against the convictions of this enlightened and merciful sovereign, that any kind of force should be laid on the consciences of men ; he is said to have exclaimed, when he heard that one of his principal cities in Hungary had been taken by the Turks, " I expected something of the kind, when I had begun to allow the sovereignty over conscience to be wrested by man from God."

This cloud, too, was then to pass away. Rudolf was able effectually to prove his tolerant principles, by bestowing on his Protestant subjects the " Majestäts-brief." This was an edict empowering them to open and maintain churches and schools wherever they would, and forbidding any violence being offered to the members of any confession on religious pretexts.

The Estates met together on this occasion, and a convocation was called, consisting of three Calixtine clergy, three from the United Brethren, three from the other evangelical confessions, and three professors of the university. These twelve men were called on to arrange the ecclesiastical affairs of the whole kingdom. The first " administrator " was chosen from the Utraquists, the rest from the other confessions indiscriminately. It was agreed that each church should have its own elder, to superintend its own concerns, who should stand in rank next to the administrator. But all was to be carried on in a spirit of brotherly union and order. The Bethlehem Church, the scene of Huss's early preaching, was given up to the United Brethren, as being more emphatically the spiritual children of Huss than the others.

The joy and exultation were general. On the very church doors might have been seen inscriptions like

the following :—" The churches are open; the lion of
Bohemia rejoices! Max has protected the faith; Rudolf
establishes it."

An agreement was drawn up, which Romanists and
Protestants were invited to sign, to the effect that all
were determined to maintain mutual union and peace.
The compact was solemnly confirmed and signed by
the emperor and his privy council.

Three chancellors alone, of the Romish Church, refused, as they declared, on conscientious grounds, to
sign the compact: these were the Chancellor Zdenko of
Lobkowitz, Slawata of Chlum, and Jaroslaw of Martiniz
Smeczansky. The last two were to play an important
part in the subsequent history of the country.

With this exception all seemed to go smoothly. It
was a time of hitherto unexampled prosperity for the
pure faith; and, indeed, it was said that at this period
scarcely one in a hundred Bohemians could be found,
who had not declared himself an adherent of evangelical
teaching. But the more pious and thoughtful men saw
ground for anxiety even in this very blaze of prosperity.
The Church of Christ can seldom bear much sunshine
without danger to her spiritual growth; and the evil
effects were already becoming apparent. A spirit of
carelessness and worldliness was beginning to mar
the purity of the reformed communities, and many
feared that a time of chastening would be needed to
awaken them from their sleep.

The hour of trial was not far off. The little cloud
was already in the horizon, which was shortly to darken
into a storm.

To explain how these troubles began, we must re-
capitulate a little.

CHAPTER IV.

RUDOLF'S power of granting religious liberty to Bohemia and Silesia had arisen partly from a division which had taken place in the empire, which indirectly strengthened the emperor's hands by weakening his subjects. In consequence of certain political combinations, Austria, Hungary, and Moravia had deserted Rudolf and chosen his brother the Archduke Matthias for their sovereign. This led to a war between the countries; the forces of the above-mentioned States had entered Bohemia in January 1608, and, advancing upon Prague, demanded not only the Hungarian crown, but also the cession of Bohemia to Matthias.

Bohemia and Silesia, however, remained faithful to the emperor; and Matthias evacuated Bohemia, having secured the crown of Hungary, and the promise of that of Bohemia at Rudolf's death.

The Bohemians, on their part, demanded and obtained from the emperor, as a reward for their faithful adherence to his cause, the promise of complete religious freedom, and full control over the consistory and the university.

Rudolf felt keenly the mortification caused by the revolt of Austria and Hungary, and the usurpation of his brother. His situation was rendered more critical by the position now assumed by Spain, which was threatening not only Bohemia, but the whole German empire, with destruction. He was anxious to take measures for the safety of his dominions; and, in selecting instruments to carry out his plans, his choice fell on two barons, on whose fidelity he considered he could fully rely. These were Kahn from Austria, and Schmidt from Bohemia. Both were of Styrian origin, and had been banished from their own country by the Archduke Ferdinand, on the occasion of the counter-reformation movement in 1600.

Rudolf summoned these barons to Prague in 1610, and laid his plans before them. He dreaded the idea of Matthias being his successor; the latter was, like himself, childless, and being entirely devoted to the Romish Church, Rudolf knew he would be persuaded by the clergy to adopt his nephew, Ferdinand, who was also their tool, as his successor.

Rudolf, on the other hand, had determined to make choice of the Archduke Leopold, Ferdinand's brother, to succeed him on the imperial throne. Though a bishop of the Romish Church, he knew Leopold had a more merciful and kindly temper than his brother, and would be more easily influenced by good counsels.

To secure his nephew from being led astray, the emperor had planned the foundation of an Order of Peace, which should be based on the great principle of freedom of conscience. The watchword of the order should be, that none who called on the name of Christ should be liable to suffer on religious grounds; and he proposed to invite all the Protestant princes, and all the Roman Catholic ones who would consent to it, to enter the order. He had already drawn up a list of these princes, and a formula of the oath to be taken on

entering the order, which he read aloud to the two
barons, at the same time giving them each as a badge a
gold chain, which he had linked with his own hand,
and ornamented with symbols of peace. He intended to
give one of these chains himself to every member of
the order.

The two barons listened with astonishment to the
emperor's discourse. He asked them if they were ready
to help him in carrying out these plans. They replied,
they knew not how they could be of any assistance.

"You can do so," rejoined the emperor, "by acting as
ambassadors for me : you, Kahn, to the German princes;
and you, Schmidt, to the chief nobility of Bohemia and
Moravia. But I must first take strong measures to
protect myself and my throne. You must first go to
Passau, to the Archduke Leopold, with credentials
written by my own hand, and lay before him my intentions. If he agrees to them, you must see that
a sufficient force is raised, and return to me with the
army."

The two barons were completely bewildered by this
speech. The scheme seemed to them nearly a hopeless
one. The emperor, perceiving their surprise, gave them
three days to consider the undertaking. At the end of
the time they promised to carry out his views to the
best of their power.

But the scheme was not destined to meet with success.
Baron Schmidt, after performing his mission in Passau,
went as delegate from the emperor to the Bohemian and
Moravian nobility, to announce to them his master's
intentions. But no one was inclined to give credit to
his representations. The whole affair was looked on as
a piece of idle ceremonial, perhaps serving as a cloak to

some intrigue. There was a simplicity and a romance about the undertaking, which to practised statesmen appeared absurd; and they feared, with some reason, a war between the rival monarchs.

Schmidt announced the failure of his embassy to the emperor, who sprang from his seat, violently irritated, and throwing open the window of his palace, from which he could look down on the city, he exclaimed: " Prague, ungrateful Prague! thou hast been renowned through my means; but now thou wouldst repulse me, thy benefactor. May the vengeance of God rest on thee and on all Bohemia!"

Baron Schmidt himself, in his old age, related this incident to the writer of this Chronicle, showing at the same time the chain which had been given him as a badge of the Order of Peace. As he drew this relic from its hiding-place, the old man said, gazing on it with tears: "The pious emperor linked this chain with his holy hands, and the malediction he pronounced on the ungrateful city has indeed fallen on us!"

Rudolf's plans all met with the same ill success. The army he had been at such pains to collect at Passau did indeed march to Prague; but Matthias was equally or better prepared on *his* side. He met the army of Passau with his troops, gained a complete victory, and was immediately proclaimed King of Bohemia. Rudolf, grieved and disappointed, died of a broken heart.

It was well for the good emperor that he did not live to see all his worst fears realised; the results, indeed, were just what he had anticipated. Matthias entered Bohemia in 1617, accompanied by his nephew Ferdinand. Being himself childless, he formally adopted

Ferdinand as his son and successor, and commanded the States of Bohemia to receive him as their king.

After having arranged for a general meeting of the States of the country, he passed into Saxony, with a view of winning the Elector's friendship for his adopted son. On his return the States met; their numbers, as he had expected and hoped, from the short notice given, and the time chosen (which was one peculiarly inconvenient to most landed proprietors), were but small.

The emperor announced his intention of adopting Ferdinand, and requested the States to receive and crown him. The States objected that so important a step could not be taken in the absence of the nobles who held fiefs under the empire. The emperor replied that Bohemia being the principal and most important country of the empire, its States could well decide in the absence of the others. The States, however, disliked the proposal, and had further objections to urge. They complained of the expression, "received a king." "It is for us," they said, "to *elect* our own sovereign, not to *accept* one chosen by others."

The emperor, however, was determined on carrying his point; and by dint of intrigues he succeeded. Ferdinand was obliged, however, to pledge himself to non-interference in religious matters. With this understanding the Bohemians consented to crown him king.

From this period the enemies of the gospel began to manifest their hostility with more confidence and determination, and the Evangelicals were threatened both secretly and openly. The Jesuits in Olmutz raised a triumphal arch, on which were depicted the Bohemian

F

lion and the Moravian eagle in chains, and beneath them a hare sleeping with open eyes, and the inscription above it,—

"I am accustomed to it."

This was a reflection on the sleepy and careless manner in which the States had suffered themselves to be taken in by the emperor and his adopted son.

And indeed it soon became apparent that Ferdinand, though he had sworn to the States of Bohemia with his lips, had sworn fealty to the pope with his heart. From this hour no pains were spared to bring about measures injurious to the Evangelicals. Their rights were violated by cunning and intrigue, and their patience was purposely tried, in order to urge them to some imprudent step which might justify retaliation. All the nobles attached to the papacy, as well as the bishops and clergy, oppressed their vassals, in direct opposition to the " Majestäts-brief." Even in Prague and in the royal free cities the same oppression was attempted. The publishers were forbidden to print anything without special permission from the chancellor; while the enemies of the gospel circulated calumnious and scurrilous writings of every kind against their opponents.

Meanwhile those pastors who were inclined to the temporising measures of the Pseudo-Hussites were secretly tampered with, to induce them to petition that the Utraquist consistory should be placed under the control of the archbishop, as in former times. Twelve of them had been persuaded to sign this, when the principal of them, Matthew Paczuda, who had been enticed by the hope of being appointed administrator, was attacked with dangerous illness, and, feeling himself at the point of death, was seized with repentance, and not only recanted, but warned his companions against the intrigues to which they had lent themselves.

This put a stop to the attempt in question; but the adherents of the papacy were not idle. The lordship of Karlstein was taken from the Count of Thurn and given to the bigoted Smeczansky, who lost no opportunity of oppressing his new vassals. The Evangelical churches in several towns were destroyed, and their inhabitants persecuted in various ways.

The States, irritated beyond endurance at these infringements of their rights, at last held a numerously attended meeting in 1618. They assembled, armed, in the citadel of the Hradschin, and in their rage against the chief fomenters of the divisions, Slawata and Martiniz, and the Secretary Fabricius, they flung them from the windows of the castle. Falling on a heap of soft earth, they were uninjured, which their friends professed to regard as a miracle. To the other party it appeared that they were preserved as a scourge for Bohemia.

This act of violence was, in fact, equivalent to a declaration of war. The States took on themselves to banish the Jesuits from the kingdom. The Bohemians then sent an embassy to the king, declaring that they had done nothing inconsistent with their respect for his majesty, but had merely punished those who had infringed the articles of the "Majestäts-brief." They entreated the emperor to assure them that he would view the matter in the same light.

But Matthias, influenced by Ferdinand, determined to have recourse to arms to punish the offence. The Bohemians put themselves on the defensive, and chose thirty directors for the time of the interregnum. Silesia and Moravia espoused the cause of Bohemia. The emperor refused to listen to those of his council who advised peaceful measures. Ferdinand is said to have answered the Bishop of Vienna, who spoke with regret of the probable devastation of the flourishing and beautiful country of Bohemia,—"We would rather have a kingdom laid waste than damned."

An imperial army was accordingly sent to attack this most prosperous and valuable portion of its sovereign's dominions, backed by a Spanish force. Such were the means to which the emperor trusted for the conversion of his refractory subjects.

But Matthias's reign was now drawing to a close. His death interrupted the proceedings, and the Bohemian States, with those of Moravia and Silesia, met to deliberate whether Ferdinand, who had been forced on them as their king against their will, and had endeavoured to destroy their privileges and liberties, could be still regarded as their lawful sovereign. They decided in the negative.

They then sent ambassadors to Frankfort, where the electors were assembled to choose a new emperor, entreating that Ferdinand, whom they refused to acknowledge as King of Bohemia, might not be elected Emperor of Germany. Their remonstrances were in vain. Ferdinand's party were too powerful among the German electors to permit the objections of one part of the empire to have any effect. He was elected Emperor of Germany, in an evil day for the cause of liberty and true religion.

The Bohemians now took the matter into their own hands. They could not prevent the ruler they so dreaded and disliked from being chosen supreme head of the "Holy Roman Empire;" but they *could* firmly refuse to acknowledge him as their king. They made choice of Frederick, Elector Palatine (who was married to the daughter of James I. of England), as King of Bohemia. He, unwisely for his own interests, accepted the offer.

Both parties now took up arms. An overwhelming force was collected by the adherents of the emperor. The Bohemians had valour, patriotism, and a just cause on their side; but against such fearful odds they had no chance. A decisive battle was fought under the walls of Prague, on the 8th of November, 1620, at Weissenberg, or the White Mountain. The newly-elected king —the "Winter King," as he was denominated—was driven from the country; the Bohemians were totally defeated, and the whole of Bohemia, Moravia, and Silesia lay crushed at the feet of the conquerors.

CHAPTER V.

THE unrighteous cause had triumphed; and now the enemies of the pure faith set themselves in right earnest to eradicate every trace of it from Bohemia.

But to accomplish this they did not follow the example of former persecuting rulers in other countries, and attack the Reformed Christians, as such, openly with fire and sword. Rome took an apparently milder but more sure way of accomplishing her purpose. Heresy was a disease which must be cured not by violent remedies, but by a wholesome and careful regimen. The heretics were not to be brought back to the fold by executions in which they might glory as martyrdoms; but they were to be wearied into obedience by slow but sure means. The harsh name of "Inquisition" was to be replaced by the milder one of " Reformation."

Accordingly a decree was passed against the Evangelicals of Bohemia, Moravia, and Silesia, which should oppress without destroying them. The instrument for carrying out this work was a Spaniard by birth, named Martin de Huerda, who had lived in Bohemia from his childhood. He must have been of humble origin, for he had begun life as a tailor; but he appears to have subsequently served in the imperial armies, and by carrying off and marrying a noble lady, the Countess Sesinia, he became ennobled. He was fortunate in war, and eventually obtained great wealth and the rank of a baron. He was said to have often boasted that he was the messenger who first brought the news of the victory at Prague to the emperor at Vienna, and that he had advised Ferdinand to leave no trace of so rebellious and heretical a people. The emperor, however, by the advice of the Duke of Bavaria, determined to try an apparently gentler mode of proceeding.

But although the steps taken against the Evangelicals in Bohemia were to be slow and gradual, it was expedient to strike terror into the rebellious party by inflicting exemplary punishment on the principal persons who had been instrumental in supporting the claims of the Elector Palatine, and opposing the election of Ferdinand as king. But, in order to punish these criminals effectively, a show of clemency was at first employed, to prevent their escaping. Accordingly, after the surrender of Prague, full pardon was promised to all who would lay down their arms and submit to the emperor.

This proclamation led many to remain in the country who might easily have escaped in the first instance. Some, indeed, either distrusting the emperor, or feeling a scruple about breaking their oath to the Elector Palatine, followed him into exile; but fifty of the most distinguished noblemen and gentlemen of Prague, whose high character and qualities had rendered them the ornaments of their country, were induced by the amnesty to remain.

At first they were lulled into security with fair promises: for more than three months nothing was spoken of but favour and mercy, and several who were in concealment actually ventured from their hiding-places on the strength of these promises.

But on the 20th of February, 1621, the private houses of the obnoxious persons were suddenly broken into, and all who were found were seized, arrested, and imprisoned in the citadel of Prague.

The next day a mandate was issued, summoning all absent and exiled nobles to appear at Prague. None of them, however, responded to the summons. They were accordingly proclaimed guilty of high treason, and their goods and lives declared forfeit.

In May, 1621, the accused nobles who were under arrest were brought before the judges and closely cross-examined. Every effort was made to urge them into a confession of crimes of which they had never been guilty. At last, Count Andreas Schlick, losing patience, tore open his vest, and, pointing to his heart, exclaimed, " Search me, and tear my body into a thousand pieces, and you will find nothing but what we have already freely avowed. We were moved to draw the sword from love of liberty and religion. But as the Lord has permitted that the emperor should gain the victory, and we should fall into his hands, His will be done !"

Otto von Loss and Herr von Budowa expressed themselves in the same manner.

Week after week passed on, while the examinations continued. None of the prisoners swerved from their convictions, none would confess crimes ; but their enemies were determined to have their blood. The pretext for condemning them was political ; but hatred to the Evangelical cause was the moving principle of their opponents. They were really martyrs to gospel truth as well as to political liberty. The emperor caused their sentences to be brought to Vienna, where he modified some of them, to give an appearance of mercy and moderation to the whole proceedings. It was a strange kind of mercy!

On the 19th of June, 1621, the sentence was finally pronounced by the judges. Twenty-seven of the prisoners were condemned to death by beheading; some of them were to lose the hand or the tongue *first*. The remainder, whose lives were spared, were condemned to exile or imprisonment for life and forfeiture of property.

The day after the condemnation, when the stadtholder, Prince Lichtenstein, was on his way to mass, he was met by a sad procession—the wives, children, and near relatives of the condemned. They threw themselves at his feet, and implored him to spare the lives of their beloved ones. The prince replied that a reprieve was now impossible, but that he might perhaps grant them the favour of being permitted a decent burial. The weeping suppliants retired, to be tortured with false hopes held out to them by greedy flatterers, who saw that they could find opportunities of plundering the distressed women of their property on pretext of being able to purchase them a pardon—hopes which soon proved to be utterly vain.

In the evening of June 21st, the condemned were allowed to have either a Jesuit confessor or a Lutheran clergyman to administer religious consolation, and give them the communion. The pastors of the Brethren's Church, to which nearly half the victims belonged, were not permitted to have access to them. The Lutherans were probably admitted out of compliment to the Elector of Saxony. But the Jesuits and Capuchins would not wait for a summons; they crowded about the prisoners, harassing them (in the words of the Chronicle) like swarms of flies. To some they held out hopes of life, and by this and other means they endeavoured to induce them to recant. But the Lord stood by His people and strengthened them. Not one wavered. The Jesuits at last left them in despair, declaring themselves clear from the blood of these obstinate heretics, who refused to accept the grace of God.

They were compelled to permit the Evangelical ministers to be called in. Six Lutheran pastors were admitted. They appear to have acted the part of true Christian ministers—consoling the prisoners with pious words, prayer, and hymns, and administering the Lord's Supper, to prepare them for their last struggle.

The members of the Brethren's Church and of the Reformed Churches received these Lutheran pastors with affection and respect as Christian brethren and ministers, assuring them they had always honoured them as such, even when some unhappy divisions had crept in and led, perhaps, to words being said on all sides which, when eternity is near, Christian men would look back to with regret.

Most of the prisoners received the Lord's Supper from these pastors ; two of them, Baron von Budowa and Otto von Loss, had some scruples, lest their receiving it from a Lutheran should be misinterpreted by enthusiastic adherents of the Brethren's Church, and therefore abstained, consoling themselves with the words, " Believe only, and thou hast eaten and drunken." But it seems to have been clearly understood on all sides that this abstinence arose from no spirit of hostility to the Lutherans, and perfect harmony was maintained among them all.

There was one other prisoner who refused the communion for a different reason. Dionysius Czerin had, in former years, at the emperor's court, relapsed into Romanism. Now, however, his former convictions had returned to him, and he seems to have bewailed his defection with deep humiliation. He was present when the Pastor Rosacius administered the communion to two of his fellow-prisoners; and when the pastor pointed out that our only well-grounded hope was in the merits and death of Christ, which would be the salvation of all who truly believed in Him, Czerin struck his breast, and exclaimed with tears, "That is my belief; and in it will I die!"

He joined in the service till the bread and wine were to be administered, and then, to the surprise of those present, instead of partaking, he drew back to one side, and kneeling, prayed earnestly by himself. When the service was over, and the others thanked the pastor, Czerin expressed his thankfulness that he had been present, and congratulated his friends that they had received so great a privilege. Rosacius expressed his surprise that he had not partaken with them. "I might, and perhaps I should have done so," said Czerin; "but—" he stopped short, struck his breast, and wept, then continued, "I am content with the grace I have received, and trust that my God will receive my deeply-troubled soul!"

It would appear likely that he had felt too much humbled by his former defection to venture to receive the communion; and however we may regard his scruples, he evidently seems to have shown a lively faith in Christ alone. He refused to the last the offices of the priests, and died with humble Christian words on his lips.

But this is anticipating; we return to the other prisoners. The condemned nobles were in the citadel; the others were all assembled in the old town-hall on the Sunday evening, the eve of their death. The Pastor Verbenius was engaged in pious discourse with them, when supper was announced by the gaoler. The prisoners looked at each other. "We need no earthly food now," they said; "but, to strengthen ourselves for the last hour, we will not refuse it."

They gathered round the table, one spreading the cloth, another pouring out water, a third arranging the plates, &c., while a fourth pronounced a blessing and helped his companions.

"It is our last meal on earth," observed one; "to-morrow we shall sit at table with Christ in His heavenly kingdom."

These words were interrupted by the mocking of an official who was present. "So you suppose the Lord will have a kitchen for you in heaven?" he said, scornfully.

The Pastor Jakesch observed that, even at the Last Supper, Christ and His disciples had been interrupted and hindered in their discourses by the presence of Judas, and it was no wonder that the same should now happen.

Dr. Hannschild, one of the condemned, declined partaking of the meal, saying, "The poor body has been long enough nourished. I need no further food."

While thus conversing, news was brought that the condemned nobles were to be taken to join their companions in the same building. The other prisoners immediately rose and went to the window, as if to receive them; and looking down on them as they passed, sang, in loud and clear tones, the forty-fourth Psalm to encourage them.

The night was passed in prayer, singing hymns, and pious conversation and mutual exhortation. They sang, amongst others, the eighty-sixth Psalm ; and when they had come to the last verse, " Show me some token for good," John Kutnaw threw himself on his knees, exclaiming, " Yea, show us a token for good, O God ! that we, Thy unworthy servants, may be strengthened by Thy grace, and our enemies put to shame." And he added, as if speaking in the name of the Lord, in an outburst of enthusiastic confidence, " Trust in Him. He *will* hear our prayer, and show us a sign to-morrow to strengthen us, and to prove that we suffer in His name." Pastor Verbenius added, " By this sign you shall know it—that death, so bitter to the wicked, shall be sweet to you."

When the morning dawned they washed and put on fresh apparel, as if preparing for a wedding. Kutnaw and some others remained for a time in earnest prayer that God would, if He saw fit, grant them a sign of His favour and their innocence before the people.

The sun rose ; and, to the astonishment of all—for there had been no rain for the last two days—a brilliant rainbow appeared, its arch spanning the whole sky. It attracted the attention of all the assembled people ; and it can scarcely be wondered at that the prisoners, as they gazed on it from their window, looked on it as a sign of promise, recalling the covenant to Noah and the bow round the throne of God in the Apocalypse. They fell on their knees and praised God aloud.

But, as the last bright colours faded away, the cannon from the tower thundered forth the signal at which the prisoners were to be led forth to die. The pastors went from one to another, with cheering words and exhortations to fight the last good fight bravely and trustfully.

And now was heard the trampling of the squadron of horse who, with a few bands of foot-soldiers, were bringing the scaffold for the last sad scene. The streets and the windows of the houses were all filled with eager spectators.

The condemned went forth, calmly and firmly, one by one. Each, as his name was called, passed out with the serene and cheerful countenance of one bidden to a festival, after taking leave of his companions, generally with some such words as these : " Dear friends, farewell ! God give you the comfort, patience, and strength of His Holy Spirit, that you may be able to bear witness to the truth you have already upheld with heart, hand, and lips, in a glorious death ! I go first, and shall see the glory of my Lord Jesus Christ ! Follow me, and we shall all look together on the face of our Father in heaven ! Our sorrows are past, and a joyful eternity awaits us ! "

The others replied : " God bless your going out, and lead you happily through the dark valley into the heavenly country ! The Lord Jesus send His holy angels to meet you ! Go forward, dear brother, into the Father's house. We follow. We shall soon meet in heavenly glory. We know in whom we have trusted."

And most abundantly was the help vouchsafed on which they trusted. None of them lost for a moment the sense of their Lord's presence ; and their earnest and heavenly words drew tears even from their judges.

The people who saw them die broke into lamentation and weeping, which was only drowned by the sound of trumpets and drums. As each passed on to his death, the pastors returned to announce it to those who remained, who praised God for His help, and prayed that they might in like manner be sustained.

The first who went forth was Count Andreas Schlick, a man more than fifty years old, and one of the most distinguished nobles of Bohemia in rank, talents, accomplishments, and valour; and his piety and calmness of demeanour were not less remarkable than his other gifts. He had been high in the service of King Frederick, and, after his defeat, had taken refuge in the 'dominions of the Elector of Saxony, whose tutor he had formerly been; but the Elector, to please his allies, had his old friend and instructor arrested and taken to prison.

When Count Schlick had heard the sentence that his body should be dismembered and exposed after death, he quietly replied, " The loss of a funeral is an easy one to bear."

On the scaffold he was harassed with entreaties from a Jesuit priest that he would recant. " You have yet time to repent, my lord," he repeated.

" Leave me in peace," replied the count.

As he stood on the scaffold, he looked up at the sun shining in the full blaze of a bright June morning. "Christ, the Sun of Righteousness," he exclaimed, " grant that I may pass through the darkness of death to Thine everlasting light!"

He walked up and down in meditation for some minutes, his face so radiant with solemn joy that the bystanders were moved to tears at the sight. He then knelt down and prayed, and received the death-blow.

His head and right hand were placed on the bridge tower, and the scaffold prepared for a new comer.

The Baron von Budowa followed, a man advanced in life, but full of animation and vigour, and richly gifted in talents and acquirements. He and Otto von Loss were officially the " Watchers of the Crown ;" and feeling that he ought to be at his post, he had returned when he had placed his wife, children, and grandchildren in safety.

" I am ready to seal the cause with my blood," he said, when arrested, to a friend who had remonstrated with him on his return. " Here I stand. My God," he added, " do with me as Thou wilt! I am weary of life. Do Thou take me, and let me not survive the ruin of my country."

On hearing a report that he had died of grief, he exclaimed, smiling, " I die of grief! Scarcely ever had I such cause for joy as now. Here is my pleasure-garden "—and he held up his Bible. " Never did such sweet nectar and ambrosia flow from it as now. No ; I live, and shall live as long as it pleases God ; and I hope that day will never come when it can be said that Budowa died of grief."

Three days before his sentence he related the following dream to his servant : He thought he was wandering in a garden, thinking anxiously on the business in hand, when a person approached him and handed him a book. He opened it, and saw that the leaves were of snow-white silk, and on one was inscribed the fifth verse of the thirty-seventh Psalm, " Commit thy way unto the Lord ; trust also in Him ; and He shall bring it to pass." As he pondered on these words, another came to him, and clothed him in a white garment. " So," said the old man, when he awoke, " I go hence clothed with the robe of righteousness, that I may see the face of God, in whom I have trusted."

The Jesuits harassed him much upon his trial. " We would show you, my lord," said one, " the way to heaven."

" The way to heaven!" said Budowa. " I know it already, through the mercy of my God."

" You are deceived," rejoined the others.

" My hope," resumed the baron, " is grounded on certain truth; for I know no way but through Him of whom it is said, ' I am the way, the truth, and the life.' "

Later, his enemies reproached him with presumption for his full assurance of safety; and a Jesuit professed to quote Scripture to the effect that man could not know whether he was the subject of grace or wrath. The baron referred to the apostle's words, "Henceforth there is laid up for me a crown of righteousness." The Jesuit objected that St. Paul said this of himself only. Budowa replied by quoting the end of the verse, "Not to me only, but unto *all* them also that love His appearing."

This silenced the objector; and Budowa asked him in what part of Scripture the words he had quoted against assurance could be found. The Jesuit was not sure. He believed they were in the Epistle to Timothy. " And you would teach me the way of salvation, and cannot show me these few words in the Bible?" said the baron. " Go, and trouble me no further."

" An honour awaits thee, my gray head," he said, on the scaffold, " to be a witness for the truth, and to wear the martyr's crown." He then prayed for the Church, his country, and his enemies, and, commending his soul to God, received the blow of the executioner.

G

Baron Christoph Henant, a celebrated traveller, was another victim. He spoke of the perils he had encountered for his country's sake, and his wonder that he should be condemned, though innocent, to a traitor's death. But he met his fate with the same pious composure and lively faith as his companions.

The Knight Caspar Caplicz, a veteran of eighty, deserves some notice. He spoke to the Pastor Rosacius, after his sentence, with tears in his eyes, but a cheerful demeanour. " My death," he said, " will be disgraceful in the eyes of the world, but glorious in God's sight ; for it is for Him I suffer."

He received the Lord's Supper devoutly, lamenting that in his youth he had followed too many of the evil practices of the world, but thanking God that He had awakened him to repentance and a new life.

" Yesterday," continued the pious old man, " my mother's sister announced to me, that if I would ask pardon and mercy from the Prince Lichtenstein, I might have my sentence commuted to imprisonment for life. But I told her I would not seek such a favour. If I asked for pardon, it would imply that I am guilty, and deserve death. And this is not the case. Tell the prince I will seek the favour of Him against whom I *have* sinned much in my former life. But to the prince I have done no harm. And if he granted me a prison instead of death, it would be a bad exchange for me. I am feeble, and weary of life. My eyes are dim, my ears dull ; I cannot walk without support. Life is burdensome to me even in freedom, and what would it be in a prison ? I am at peace with God," he added, later, " and fear no man. My flesh and heart fail, but God is my portion for ever. Sinner as I am, I am cleansed through the blood of my Redeemer. Let my hour come when it may, I am ready."

As he arrayed himself with unusual care, and in his most costly apparel, he observed to a companion, "I am putting on my marriage garments." "The righteousness of Christ is the true clothing for the inner man," said the other. "I know it," rejoined the old knight; "but for the honour of my heavenly Bridegroom I wish also to be outwardly dressed in festive garments."

He was now summoned to the scaffold. "In God's name," he replied; "I have waited long enough." Supported by his servants—for he was too feeble to walk alone—he moved slowly to the place of execution, after taking leave of his friends. As he had to descend some stairs on his way, he said, "My God, give me strength, that I may not stumble, and cause my enemies to mock me!"

The old man was too stiff and weak to kneel without great difficulty. He begged the executioner to give the stroke as soon as he was able to place himself on his knees, as he could not remain long in that position. "Lord Jesus, into Thy hands I commend my spirit," were his last words.

Prokop Dworzercky showed the same calm faith and resolution. "I had a long struggle with the old Adam the whole of last night," he said to the pastor; "but, God be praised! through His help I have gained the victory. My Saviour has died and risen again, to be Lord of the living and dead; and I know that my soul will also be victorious, and my body be raised up and made like to His glorious body."

On the scaffold he turned to the imperial judges. "Tell the emperor," he said, "we must now submit to his unjust sentence; but *he* will have to suffer a more severe and more just judgment from God." He gave his purse to a friend, begging him to give its contents to the poor. Then taking a gold coin, with the stamp of the Elector Palatine Frederick upon it, from his neck, he gave it to a bystander, saying, "I entreat you, if my beloved king should again be restored to his throne, give him this, and tell him I wore it to my last hour from love to him, and now willingly give my life for God and my king."

Otto von Loss was a man of acute mind and high resolve. He had filled situations of trust under both the Emperor Rudolf and King Frederick.

When he learned that his body was to be exposed and dismembered after death, he said, "I have been among barbarous nations, but such vengeance as this I never witnessed! Well, they may send a portion of my body to Rome, another to Spain, another to the Turks, and another beyond the sea, as they please. I believe my Saviour will gather together all, and will clothe me again with flesh. With my eyes I shall see Him, with my ears hear Him, with my mouth praise Him, and with my heart rejoice in Him for ever."

When Rosacius, after accompanying Dworzercky to the scaffold, returned to the prison, Otto rose to meet him in a kind of rapture, exclaiming, " How I rejoice to meet you, man of God, that I may tell you what has happened to me! I was sitting on this seat, sorrowing because I could not have a minister of my own Church to give me the Lord's Supper after our fashion, and I began to regret, as I do now, that I did not join the others and receive it from you. While full of these thoughts I fell asleep for a moment, and my Saviour appeared to me, saying, 'My grace is sufficient for thee: with My blood I will strengthen thee;' and He let a drop of His blood fall on my heart. At the touch I awoke, and now I feel myself wonderfully strengthened and refreshed in my soul."

He then broke forth into an ecstasy of prayer and thanksgiving. "I thank Thee, O my Saviour!" he exclaimed, "that Thou hast given me such consolation, and hast counted me worthy to feel this assurance of Thy grace. Now I understand these words, 'Believe, and thou hast eaten and drunken.' Ah, I feel now that I die with joy; death has no terrors for me."

When he was called to go to the scaffold, he asked Rosacius to accompany him. "Willingly," replied the good pastor. "You have just seen the Lord Jesus in a dream," he added; "but soon you will see Him among the blest, as He is in His glory." "I am sure of it," replied Von Loss. "He is coming to meet me with His angels, to lead me to the heavenly marriage feast, where I shall drink of the cup of joy for ever. Oh! I know death will not separate me from Him."

On the scaffold he appeared absorbed in prayer; then suddenly raising his eyes, he exclaimed, "I see the heavens opened!" and pointed to the sky, where even others thought they saw an unusual brightness of glory, as of an angelic host in battle array. Commending his soul to his Saviour, he joyfully received the death-stroke.

Boleslaus von Michalowicz showed the same spirit. He was full of eager longing for martyrdom; and when his companions were led out, one by one, before him, he feared he was forgotten, and exclaimed sorrowfully, "My God! what is this? Thou knowest I have given myself into Thy hands! Ah! look on Thy poor servant, and take me quickly!"

The officer of justice now summoned him. He rose joyfully, and with words of fervent trust in his Saviour laid his head on the block.

Another victim, Tobias Hiffel, a burgher of Prague, a man of gentle and mild temper and eminent piety, seemed depressed but resigned throughout his imprisonment. "I have received good at the Lord's hands," he said; "shall I not also receive evil? I thank the mercy of my God, who has allowed me to be the companion of these distinguished men, and share with them the crown of martyrdom."

When he was led forth to the scaffold he raised his hands to heaven, with tearful eyes, and said, "When my Saviour died for me, He said, 'Father, not My will, but Thine be done!' How I, a worm of the dust, shall I desire to resist His will? God forbid! See, my God, I come obediently to Thee; have mercy on me, and cleanse me from my sins, that not a spot or wrinkle may be found on me, but I may appear purified in Thy presence!"

The pastor consoled him with promises from the Scriptures. "A little while," he replied, "and the Lord will wipe away all tears from my face, and all sorrow and anguish shall be changed into everlasting joy!" With these words he rose, subdued, but calm and trustful, and expired with prayer on his lips.

Jessenius, a Hungarian physician, celebrated for learning and talent, and who had held high offices under several princes, received one of the severest of the sentences. When he heard of the dismemberment after death, he said, as if prophetically, "The time will come when our heads, now so shamefully exposed and made a spectacle, will receive honourable interment."

This did actually happen.   During the short triumphant career of Gustavus Adolphus, the Elector of Saxony entered Prague with a victorious army, and the heads of the martyrs were taken down from the tower of the bridge, and solemnly interred in the presence of a large concourse of people, and a funeral sermon preached by a pastor recalled from banishment.

The Jesuits made many efforts to induce Jessenius to recant.   While they were dwelling on the efficacy of good works, he turned to them, and observed, " Gentlemen, if I were to come over to your belief, there would not be time left for me to complete so great a collection of works of merit as you demand, and then what would become of my soul ? "

" My dear Jessenius," replied a Jesuit, " the *will* to do them is all that is needed ; and then, if you die this moment, we can promise that you will go straight to heaven ! "

" Then what becomes of your purgatory, which was intended for those who did not fill up the prescribed tale of good works ? " asked Jessenius.

The Jesuits were silenced, and withdrew ashamed. Jessenius was condemned to lose his tongue before his head was struck off.   " It is hard," he observed, " to be so cruelly robbed of the tongue with which I have faithfully served so many princes ; but I shall not be dumb in the resurrection."

He patiently submitted to this cruel mutilation, and then fell on his knees and prayed with stammering lips, till the executioner's death-blow freed his soul.

" I shall not die, but live, and declare the works of

the Lord in the land of the living," said Christoph Roker, another of the martyrs, as he calmly prepared for execution; and, commending his spirit to the Lord, he laid his head on the scaffold.

Another repeated with lively faith the words of Simeon, "Lord, now lettest Thou Thy servant depart in peace." They were his last words.

Nicolas Wodniansky, an aged man, was encouraged by his son John, a burgher of Prague. "Father," he said, weeping bitterly, "if hopes of life are held out to you on condition of falling from the faith, think on the fidelity we owe to Christ." "My son," replied the father, "I rejoice that you urge me to stedfastness; but how can you think I should give way? Rather let me warn you to be firm in treading in my steps, and keep your sisters and brothers and children in the same stedfastness."

John was conducted to a different gallows from that on which his friend Kutnaw and his father-in-law were to suffer. At first this grieved him; but on being reminded of the glory of suffering shame for Christ's name, he was cheered, and met his fate with serene composure.

Kutnaw, whose prayer for a sign from God has been already mentioned, was the youngest of the victims (he was scarcely forty); but in his lofty enthusiasm and joyful firmness he almost surpassed them all. A Jesuit who had vainly endeavoured to convert him said to one of his colleagues, "These men are as hard as rocks; they cannot be moved." "Yes," said Kutnaw, "you are right. We are founded on Christ, a Rock that shall never be moved."

He was condemned to be hanged, not beheaded. "I

know not," he said, " how the executioner will deal with
me, and I care not; I only regret that my blood will
not mingle with that of my companions." He embraced
his friends warmly; and seeing tears in the eyes of some
who were to remain in prison, he encouraged them,
saying, "It is but a little while, and we shall all be
together in glory."

He sang a Bohemian hymn as he approached the
scaffold. His last words were, " I have committed no
crime; I die because I have been faithful to my country
and the gospel. God forgive my enemies; they know
not what they do; and then, Lord Jesus, have mercy
on me, and receive my spirit!"

His father-in-law, Sussicky, who was nearly of the
same age, was hanged beside him. The words in Gala-
tians, "Cursed is he that hangeth on a tree," had been
very distressing to him; but the Pastor Verbenius had
pointed out to him that Christ, having been made a
curse for us, had abolished the curse and condemnation.
This cheered his soul, and his peace and joy never left
him afterwards. The others all met their fate in the
same spirit. Some expired singing hymns of praise,
others exhorting their companions with words of faith
and hope.

Those who escaped capital punishment had, perhaps,
more to suffer. One of them was condemned to have
his tongue pierced with a sharp spear, being thus fastened
to the gallows, in which torture he remained two hours.
He was then sent back to prison, where he remained
four years, and was afterwards banished. This cruel
punishment was inflicted merely because he had been
appointed to welcome King Frederick, when he entered
Prague, with a greeting in the name of the citizens, and

had saluted him with good wishes when he left. Several others were beaten severely with rods, imprisoned, and banished.

The Moravian nobles who had taken part with the elector were imprisoned for four years, and their goods confiscated.

On the 28th of June, 1621, a week after the execution of the prisoners at Prague, the property of all who had been put to death or banished, or who had taken flight in the first instance, was formally confiscated.

CHAPTER VI.

THE rest of the nobility who had had any share in the late proceedings remained in painful suspense, expecting their share of the punishment. It came very soon. In the following year a mandate was published proclaiming a general pardon for past offences against the government. But all these political offenders must forfeit to the crown a portion of their estates, to help the emperor, as it was alleged, to pay the expenses of the war.

This so-called pardon, therefore, was really a heavy fine. It amounted in fact to more—to a general spoliation. All the offenders were ordered to make an estimate of their property, with the view of arranging for the payment of the subsidy. But, to secure the full amount being paid, they were compelled to deliver up the whole of their property in land, houses, castles, villages, &c.; and in return they received a paper or bond for the portion which they were supposed to have restored to them. In this paper they were directed to await the decision of the Imperial Chamber in order to receive back the remainder of their property.

But, on one pretence or another, the whole was in this way withheld from them. Some retired to the towns, some undertook the superintendence of their former property, to support themselves, others found an asylum with Romanist friends and relatives; a few succeeded, by private interest, or by making a fresh purchase, in recovering their own or their wives' property. Moveable property was often included in this spoliation; and some were even compelled to alight from their carriages, to give up their horses and the boxes of valuables they were carrying.

Many were included in this vexatious measure who had taken no open part against the government; some even who, from sickness or infirmity, would have been utterly unable to do so if they had been willing.

Means were found to seize the property of those who had money lent at interest. The castles, estates, and villages thus seized were divided among the Italian, Spanish, and German favourites of the emperor.

But the vengeance of the conquerors was not limited to the nobility and richer inhabitants. It was to extend by degrees to all—warlike or peaceful, high or low, rich or poor—who followed the doctrines of the Reformed Churches.

The first measure passed against the Evangelicals generally was a decree, issued in the second year after the battle of Weissenberg, and against the Anabaptists of Moravia. This sect possessed about forty-five meeting-houses, which also served as dwelling-places to many private families among them. According to the principles they then held, they had their goods in common; they lived peaceably, were a burden on no one, and carried on their various callings quietly and diligently.

In the autumn of 1622 these humble and peaceful Christians were all banished, on the pretext of their having shown hospitality to King Frederick when he passed through Bohemia. It was just the time of vintage; but there must be no delay; these homeless

families must leave their houses, and fields, and vine-
yards loaded with ripening grapes to be gathered by
other hands.   They placed their families and moveables
in some hundred waggons; and unarmed, according to
their principles, they quietly removed into the neighbouring states of Hungary and Transylvania, where
they found a safe and peaceful asylum, and were spared
the sufferings which their countrymen and brethren in
the faith were soon to encounter.

The next step was to endeavour to expel the
"Picards," or members of the Brethren's Church, and
those of the Calvinistic or Reformed communions; but
this was not easy at first to accomplish.   Many nobles
of unimpeached loyalty to the emperor belonged to each
of these communions, and some pretext must be found
for banishing them, which was a more difficult task
than in the case of the poor unprotected Anabaptists.

Then, again, the members of the Calvinist and
Lutheran communions could not always be easily distinguished; and, finally, the time was not come when
it would be safe to offend the Protestant princes of
Germany.   But the enemies of the Reformed faith
were numerous, zealous, and united; and they were
prepared to bide their time.   It was determined, as a
preliminary step, to place all on the list of condemned,
and then to await a fitting occasion for carrying out the
plan of action.

One of the principal actors in this well-laid scheme
was a Jesuit of low origin, named Paul Michna.   His
zeal for the house of Austria and the cause of the pope,
and his active spirit of intrigue, had raised him to rank
and influence; he had been among the first consulted
as to the measures to be taken.   He advised delay,

because, as he said, the banished nobles might take a good deal of property out of the country with them. The first step must be, therefore, to deprive them of their goods.

In accordance with this plan, after the surrender of Prague, the soldiers had been permitted to plunder the houses of the nobles and rich citizens; and, as much valuable property had been stored up in the city, as in a place of safety, the army reaped a rich harvest.

Heavy contributions were then levied on the inhabitants; and they were compelled to support the army for a considerable time at their own expense. Some few were induced to renounce the faith, in hopes of being freed from these impositions. Promises were made to that effect, which were not kept; and on the sufferers complaining, the Jesuits were ready with their answer:

"We are treating you," they said, "like children or fools, who must be coaxed with kind words and promises, which we may not choose to keep, to give up a knife or other dangerous weapon they may have laid hold of. We have done this in care for your souls; and now you should show your gratitude to the conqueror by more zealously contributing your money and support to the soldiers."

The kingdom had been, by this means, nearly stripped of gold and silver. The emperor then issued a coinage made of a mixture of silver and gold, which was widely circulated, that the common people, ignorant of such matters, might be deceived into thinking it genuine; but the soldiers would be satisfied with nothing less than good coin. The value of gold and silver increased tenfold. In the year 1624 the emperor passed an edict to lower it, and declared that each coin should be worth only a tenth of its former value.   It can easily be imagined what general distress was occasioned by this oppressive edict.

At last, after every corner had been searched and plundered, an order was passed to relieve debtors by cancelling every debt which had been voluntarily incurred during the rebellion, and excusing the interest of part of the principal of what had been lent before the war, while the payment of the remainder was to be postponed for ten years.   Thus the prosperity of the whole kingdom was ruthlessly sacrificed, in order to carry out the persecuting principles of the Popish and Imperial party.

But to return to the course of events following the battle at Prague.   The emperor and his party had now completely despoiled their opponents.   The next step was to drive them to desperation by insults and persecution.   No expression of scorn or mockery, in writing, printed books and pamphlets, caricatures, and insolent jesting words, was spared.   But this was only general persecution, and it could not satisfy the malice of the enemies of the truth.

A so-called "Reformation Committee" of monks and Jesuits was formed, whose office it was to go through the various districts, towns, and villages of the country, pointing out the evils of heresy in the blackest colours, praising the Romish Church, and, by flattery, promises, threats, or ill usage, to entice or frighten all into recanting and embracing the Romish faith.

Whoever wished to leave the country must first obtain a passport; but, before receiving it, he was harassed and pressed with vexatious questions and exhortations by the Jesuits. If he refused to conform to the Romish Church, he was invited at least to consent to receive instruction. Anyone who yielded to this was in the power of the priests, and by daily harassing and urging they too often gained their point. Whosoever refused, was banished forthwith. Many submitted in order to gain time to arrange their affairs; but if, after receiving the prescribed course of instruction, they declared their belief unchanged, they were accused of despising his imperial majesty, and ran considerable risk of being punished for high treason.

A systematic persecution of the Evangelical pastors of Bohemia followed. A foretaste of this had been already given in the cruelty with which all such were treated who had the misfortune to fall into the hands of the imperial soldiers. A few instances may suffice.

Wenzel Wotic, the aged pastor of Bistricz in Moravia, was found by a Polish regiment in the emperor's service lying sick in bed; he was seized, robbed, and shot dead. But his fate was a more merciful one than that of many of his brethren, who, on pretence of being supposed to conceal treasure, were put to the most horrible tortures to force them to disclose it. Several were actually burned alive with their wives, and others put to deaths too fearful to describe.

One of these pastors, however, had a most remarkable escape. He was arrested in his house by fifteen horsemen, who bound his hands, head, and feet tightly with cords, and laid him on the ground, to await further tortures on the morrow. While he lay in this condition he engaged in earnest prayer, and adopted as his own the language of the psalm, "In Thee, O Lord, have

I put my trust." Just as he had ended the psalm, he felt, to his great astonishment, the cords loosening round his hands and feet, and presently found himself freed. He rose softly, opened the door, and passed by the guard. Three soldiers were keeping watch, one of whom held the door-latch in his hand; but all seemed as if stupefied, and either sleepy or unable from the noise of a violent tempest which had begun to rage to hear the sound of his footsteps. He passed them un-molested, reached the city gate, and was then recognised by a soldier on guard. But fortunately the man was a Bohemian, and was won over by entreaties to let his countryman pass; and the prisoner escaped to a place of safety.

In the beginning of the year 1621 six articles were laid before the General Evangelical Consistory, to which all the pastors of Prague, Bohemian and German, of all three confessions, were required to sub-scribe. These articles amounted, in fact, to a complete renunciation of the Reformed faith. The pastors were to be reordained by the archbishop, to restore all the ancient ceremonies, to separate from their wives, or to request, as a favour, that their marriages might be tolerated.

The pastors unanimously refused to violate their con-sciences by signing these articles. Their enemies had then recourse to other means. On the 13th December, 1621, an edict was passed, in the name of Prince Lichtenstein, laying the whole blame of the rebellion on the clergy of Prague : they were represented as enemies to the public peace, and commanded to leave the city in three days, and the kingdom in eight days, never to return on any pretext, on pain of death.

In this manner all the Bohemian pastors were banished from Prague, and their churches given up to the Jesuits. We can imagine the universal dismay, distress, and anguish with which these Christian ministers parted from their flocks.

CHAPTER VII.

THE Bohemian-speaking inhabitants of Prague, deprived of their own ministers, now flocked to the German services, which they could in some degree understand; for the German pastors, out of regard to the Elector of Saxony, were not immediately subjected to the same treatment as the Bohemians.

But the indulgence shown them was only temporary. The Jesuits, seeing the German services so numerously attended, resolved rather to incur the displeasure of the elector than to allow this abuse, as they considered it, to continue. They did not, indeed, speak of "banishing" the German pastors, but only graciously *dismissing* them; the difference, however, was only nominal.

In spite of the protests of the elector, the pastors were compelled to depart from Prague on the 29th of October, 1622. They were accompanied by a multitude of Bohemians as well as Germans, to whom they preached farewell sermons in the fields, while the air resounded with the loud weeping and lamentations of their auditors.

The next step was to extend the edict of banishment to the pastors throughout the whole of Bohemia. This work was commenced in the same year, and after a fashion quite characteristic of the whole work. The " Reformation Commissioners," as they were called, as if in mockery, passed from city to city to carry out the decree.

Michna, at the head of a troop of horse, entered the church of Schlan; it was a festival day, and the pastor, Johann Kaupilius, a man of learning and talent as well as piety, was reading the gospel at the communion-table. A soldier was directed to impose silence on him. The minister continued calmly to read on. Michna stepped forward, drew his sword, and exclaiming, ".Shameless preacher, cease your babbling!" struck the Bible out of his hands.

The pastor's reply was to raise his hands and eyes to heaven, with the words, " Woe unto you! for ye shut the gates of heaven, and will not suffer men to enter in! I am ready," he continued, " to suffer this and more for the sake of my Lord Jesus Christ." " *Your* Lord!" cried a soldier, repeating the sacred name again and again in mocking tones. " *We* have the emperor for *our* lord!"

The people were struck with horror at the blasphe-mous words, and many wept aloud. The principal members of the town-council now came forward, and promised that their pastor would appear when he was summoned, but protested against any violence being shown him. The commissary first threatened to im-prison Kaupilius; but, at the entreaty of some ladies in the city, he consented to set him free on condition of his departing within three days.

Three years afterwards, the faithful pastor died of the plague in his place of banishment. On his death-bed he had a remarkable dream, which he related to his friends. He thought he was standing in a library of choice books. As he examined them, a small volume caught his eye, which bore this title in Latin, in letters of gold : *It is good that the righteous should be sacrificed : they shall at last receive the crown.* He felt moved with ardent love to the book, and placed it under his left arm, to study it at leisure. But he awoke at the same moment, roused probably by the pain which marked the presence of the fatal plague-spot under the arm where he had held the book in his dream.

He had written and published several works during his exile, manifesting the same ardent zeal for truth which had characterized his life.

By degrees the other towns and villages of Bohemia were in like manner deprived of their preachers. The churches were filled, in their stead, with Romish priests ; and, as a sufficient number could not be easily found on the spur of the moment, monks from Poland were brought, and others from other places, many of them of the lowest and most depraved character, whose vices created general scandal.

By August, 1624, all the Evangelical ministers in Bohemia—Lutheran, Picard, and Reformed, German and Bohemian—were driven from the country.

Some returned, from time to time, in secret, and endeavoured to collect their hearers in hiding-places among the forests and mountains, where they instructed them and administered the sacraments. But when this became known to their enemies, a fresh edict was obtained from the emperor in July, 1625, threatening with punishment all who should harbour a banished preacher, and offering rewards to those who should betray the hiding-place of any such. Several preachers were seized and thrown into prison, where every effort was made by the Jesuits, by threats and promises, to induce them to recant.

Some were, unhappily, driven by fear and suffering to renounce their faith; but, by the grace of God, the greater number of those who had fallen into the hands of the enemy remained faithful. Some few were set free after a long imprisonment, on condition of quitting the country, never to return on pain of death; others were compelled, in addition, to pay heavy fines.

Matthias Ulicky, the deacon of Czaslau, returned in 1627 from banishment in order to visit his sick wife. He was found in a place of concealment, arrested and brought to Czaslau, where Michna and others of the reigning powers were assembled. It was found on inquiry that he had been during the last three years concealed in the neighbourhood, and had encouraged many of his former flock to remain faithful to the truth. He was told that his life might be spared if he conformed to Rome; but, sustained by a strength not his own, he declared boldly that he held his office not from the emperor, but from Christ, and had never laid it down at the command of men, and that he could never renounce his faith. He was asked if he celebrated the Lord's Supper "in the Calvinistic fashion" (that is, in both kinds). "I do so, in accordance with the example and command of Christ," he replied.

Kostschnik, one of the inquisitors, tried to urge him to confess he had taken part against the emperor. "Do not burden your conscience," he said, "by denying your crime." "I have cared for my conscience better than you have for yours," replied the pastor. The justice of this reproach so preyed on the mind of the inquisitor that his agitation brought on an illness which eventually proved fatal.

The pastor was led to execution. As he went, the

judge proclaimed, with a loud voice, "This man is guilty of sedition!" "No!" replied the prisoner, raising his voice; "I am suffering for Christ's truth."

Professor John Aquila attempted to hand him a hymn-book as he passed out of the city gate, for which he was struck with a stick and driven away. Ulicky, however, had a well-stored memory, and sang through the seventieth psalm and several hymns; but drums and trumpets were employed to drown his voice. "To-day," he exclaimed, on the scaffold, "my soul will be with Christ!" With these words he knelt down, commended his soul to the Saviour, and patiently awaited the blow of the executioner. His right hand was first struck off, because with it he had held the cup to the laity; he was then beheaded.

All the Evangelical ministers were thus driven from the country; and any who harboured them, under whatever pretext, were liable to severe punishment.

One brave man, the Baron von Zierotin, dared openly to remonstrate against the injustice of being deprived of the ministrations of his pastor. He went himself to Vienna, and laid his complaint before the emperor. "I cannot conscientiously do otherwise," was Ferdinand's reply. "But I, too," said the baron, "am pledged to God by my conscience, and I entreat your majesty not to compel me to violate it." "I will not force you to violate your conscience," said the emperor; "but I cannot suffer you to retain your minister." "But I cannot dispense with Divine service," said the baron, "and for that I require a pastor."

His determination actually gained the day. Without obtaining the permission of the emperor, he persisted not only in retaining his chaplain, Paul Hronow, but, like Obadiah of old, sheltered many others (amongst them, the President of the Bohemian Brethren in Moravia, John Lanetius, a venerable man of more than seventy) in places of concealment, and provided them with food.

Hronow held a service in the baron's castle not only for the retainers and vassals, but for all the neighbours who held the same faith, who were admitted freely without fear of consequences. Some other firm-minded men of rank followed this good example, till a general sentence of banishment put a stop to every effort of the kind.

But in July, 1627, an imperial mandate appeared, declaring that heresy was the root of all the miseries under which Bohemia suffered, and that the emperor's conscience would not permit him to suffer any to remain with this taint upon him. Six months were granted, during which the higher classes were to be allowed time and opportunity for being instructed in the Romish faith, and the " Reformation Commissioners " were appointed to carry out these arrangements. At the end of the six months' probation, all who remained obstinate were to sell their property to Roman Catholics, and depart from the kingdom.

And now was come the sifting time which should show who were really firm in the faith. Those who felt their religion to be a matter which concerned their inmost hearts, and loved their Lord well enough to give up all for His sake, went at once into exile.

Some tried to move the emperor to compassion, and endeavoured to obtain a respite, making all kinds of excuses for not following his directions. Some even succeeded in purchasing false testimonials that they had confessed and attended mass, and thus evaded the decree.

The more upright and devoted left their homes and inheritances, and passed into other countries with their wives and children. Most of them emigrated into Silesia, Poland, and Hungary. Among these exiles was the pious old Baron von Zierotin, who could easily have obtained leave to stay, if he would have given up Protestant worship; but he was one to whom his faith was dearer than all earthly possessions or comfort. He was obliged to sell his estates at half their price, and went, with the emperor's sanction, to Breslau in Silesia.

But even in banishment these exiles were not left in peace. In 1628 they were informed by an imperial missive that they must not remain in any of the provinces belonging to the emperor. They were to be liable to punishment if they did not go entirely out of his dominions.

An attempt was made to compel all Romanists who had Protestant wives to send them out of the country; but some of the highest of the nobility were in this case, and, not choosing to part from their wives, they made so determined a resistance to this decree that they were at last permitted to retain them, on the condition that these ladies should withdraw from all festivities and public ceremonies, give the precedence to Romanists whenever they did appear, and at the death of their husbands immediately leave the country.

The Evangelical tutors and schoolmasters, and all who took part in the instruction of youth, were banished, and it was penal for parents to have their children instructed by any but a Romanist. Severe penalties were laid on all who should infringe a multitude of new regulations relative to the Romish ceremonial; and many chief citizens of Prague and other towns were banished on frivolous pretexts.

The Reformation Commissioners were indefatigable in finding means of tormenting or frightening men into giving up their faith.   In 1625, on Easter Eve, all the citizens of Leitmeritz were summoned by name to appear at the sermon and mass on Easter Sunday. Every one who attended was to receive a ticket with his name signed by the priest, and a fine was imposed on all who should fail to appear.   But the summons was not responded to, or only in part.

A numerous body of soldiers was then quartered on the town, and placed in the houses of the refractory, and every means used to annoy and terrify them into submission.   After a year of these efforts an edict was passed, banishing all who would not conform to the Romish religion ; and, to the honour of Leitmeritz, it must be said that the larger number of the Evangelical inhabitants preferred emigration to apostasy.

At Königsgratz the Croatian soldiers were called in to help the Romish teachers, and actually endeavoured with drawn swords to force the people into joining a procession.   But this only produced general alarm, tumult, and confusion. The Reformation Commissioners called in further military aid, and applied individually to the principal citizens to induce them to submit.

One of the first so addressed was Nicolas Acontius, a physician residing in the neighbourhood, who had been for several years completely laid up with gout. The archdeacon, accompanied by Strauss, the captain of the guard, came to visit the sick man, and asked him " if he would not now become a Catholic ? "   " As long as I have no reasons which can. convince my mind, I dare not act against my conscience," replied the courageous old man.

"We cannot allow your deceitful tricks any longer," said the archdeacon, angrily.

"There can be no deceit where the eye, heart, and conscience are single," replied Acontius.

The priest lost his temper completely. "We shall never bring this town to reason," he cried, "till three or four heads have been cut off!"

"If you find my head is in your way," replied the old physician, calmly, "and you have a right to it, you can strike it off at once. I would rather have this poor half-decayed body cut in pieces than violate my conscience."

The archdeacon started up in a rage and rushed out. Captain Strauss, as he followed him, said in a low voice to Acontius, "Sir, the world is wide; a way of escape will be opened to you."

The gates of the city were now closed, and the citizens severely threatened, to enforce compliance. The timid promised to allow themselves to be instructed; those who refused were arrested and placed in confinement. Every stronghold, and even the cellars and anterooms of the town-hall, were crowded with prisoners. The houses were filled with soldiers, who were ready to do their part in tormenting the unfortunate inmates.

Most of the prisoners at last lost their courage, and asked for a respite to receive instruction, thus giving themselves up into the hands of the enemy. Twenty-eight alone among the citizens had the firmness to give up all for conscience' sake, and go into banishment with their families. Acontius joined this little band, though so feeble and suffering that it was with difficulty he could enter the carriage which was to convey him to Poland. He survived his exile nine years, bearing his bodily sufferings with cheerful patience, and at last peacefully fell asleep in Christ.[1]

At Bidschow, some miles from Königsgratz, Don Martin de Huerda was employed to terrify the inhabitants into compliance. Their spokesman, John Kolacznich, said, in the name of his companions: "It does not lie in the power of any one to forget in an hour what he has been learning throughout his whole life; and one could not cast away what he had held as Divine truth, unless better doctrine could be taught him from God's Word."

Huerda, beside himself with rage, started from his seat, flew on the speaker, and beat him furiously with the stick he held in his hand. He also ordered the keeper of the town-hall to be called, and, foaming with rage, commanded him to drive Kolacznich out of the town. His colleagues, terrified by this violence, consented to allow themselves to receive instruction. Some tried to save their consciences by flight, and sent their wives secretly before them with their little property; but the plan was discovered, the women pursued, robbed, brought back and put in prison, whence they were not released till they and their husbands had consented to become Roman Catholics, which, alas! they at last did.

At Saaz, another considerable town, a number of

---

[1] It is impossible to read of these cruelties at Königsgratz without feeling as if there was something like a very solemn retribution in the circumstance that this very place was, two centuries later, the scene of Austria's most signal defeat. It is not the only instance in modern history in which the spot where a great wickedness has been perpetrated has been made, like Naboth's vineyard, the scene of righteous retribution.

Bibles and Evangelical books were seized and burned. The soldiers were quartered on the people, and made havoc of their goods. A meeting was then called in the town-hall, and Don Martin de Huerda declared that all who would consent to go to mass and confession should be freed from the burden of the soldiers quartered on them, but that all who resisted should have double burdens laid upon them.

The majority of the members of the council seemed paralysed with terror at the threats of the Spaniard.

One of the presidents, Wenzel Wisocky, however, summoned courage to address Huerda. He spoke calmly and moderately, and dwelt on the rights of conscience. Don Martin started up furiously, boxed the ears of the speaker several times, and abused him in the grossest terms. He then called for iron chains, and commanded them to be fastened on the hands and feet of Wenzel, while a thicker chain was placed round his neck and attached again to his hands, so as to keep him bent forwards. He remained in prison three weeks in this painful and cramped posture, with no food but bread and water. None of his own friends were permitted access to him, and the Jesuits harassed him night and day.

They threatened him with death, but this he preferred to recanting. They then declared he was possessed with a devil, and ordered his chains to be drawn tighter. The poor man, almost distracted with bodily and mental suffering, at last consented to confess. His yielding seems to have been almost involuntary; and as soon as the pressure was taken off, he showed his real earnestness of belief by giving up his home and country to worship according to his conscience. Being allowed to go to some mineral baths to recruit his broken health, he took advantage of the permission, and left his country never to return.

More than a hundred citizens of Königsgratz escaped secretly, leaving all they possessed. Many of these were men of the highest rank. One of them, Herr von Kraliz, was married to a lady of great wealth; but both husband and wife were prepared to leave all for the truth's sake. The lady abandoned her property, escaped through an underground sewer, joined her husband with much difficulty, and followed him into exile.

Some fugitives were driven, by extreme want in the land of their exile, to return and endeavour to seek some help from their native country. But too often they were seized and imprisoned. Two citizens of Saaz fell in this way into the hands of Huerda, who tormented them till their health and almost their reason were destroyed. They were at last set free when half dead with suffering.

Another persecutor, no less cruel than Huerda, was Zdenko, Lord of Kolowrath. He was sent by Prince Lichtenstein with a troop of horse to the town of Rokycan. After loading the peaceful citizens with the vilest abuse and mockery, he laid before them a paper with three lists. The first contained the names of all who were already Romanists. These were but six in number, all of whom had renounced the Evangelical faith. The second contained those who were ready to become Roman Catholics in a fortnight; and the third those who, as Zdenko expressed it, resisted God and the emperor.

The citizens were compelled to sign this register. The number of the recusants was by far the greatest; and Zdenko loaded them with curses, declaring they were worthy only of the wheel and the cross in this world, and hell in the next.

The next day was St. Thomas's Day. Zdenko ordered them all to appear in the church, and himself set them the example by receiving the consecrated wafer at mass. After dinner he again caused the bells to be rung, to collect the people into the church; but, on entering himself, he found the monks and other faithful worshippers unpunctual, and the others remaining absent. The church was empty. Transported with rage, he rushed into the market-place, entered the streets and the private houses, and drove all he could find to the church with a stick!

On re-entering the church, he found there a leading citizen, named John Streic, well known as a firm Calvinist. Snatching a cudgel from a peasant who stood by, he drove Streic to the altar, cursing him as he went, because, as he said, he had placed himself on the list of the reprobates by refusing confession.

Streic mildly begged him to consider the sacredness of a place of worship, and to moderate his violence. Zdenko replied by a shower of furious blows on his head, face, and hands. Streic threw himself on his knees, and prayed for help. At last, when the tyrant saw the blood flowing in streams from his victim, he cried, " Be off, with your Calvinist blood!" and turned from him.

The pious and brave sufferer quietly left the church and when met by some who asked what had happened to him, he meekly replied, " I have shed my blood at the altar; but it was for His sake who shed His blood for me in far greater abundance."

Zdenko turned to the other burghers, and endeavoured to compel them to confess. With oaths and curses, he struck some, spat in the face of others; and, seizing on one venerable old man, Wenzel Krok, one of the most highly-respected of the citizens, he tore his gray beard, and scattered the hairs over the church.

Returning home, he sent for Streic, and threatened him with a fearful end if he did not resolve the next day to submit. Streic wisely determined not to await the decisive day, but fled in the middle of the night. He was compelled to leave his wife, his children, and his aged mother behind him. The count revenged himself by ordering his property to be confiscated and his wife imprisoned.

How many of the citizens at last gave way we are not informed; but those who did were compelled to sign a paper declaring they had recanted and joined the Church of Rome of their own free will, and that they thanked the blessed Virgin and Count Zdenko for the salvation of their souls!

Zdenko was eventually recalled to Vienna, where his zeal for the Romish Church did not save him from being arrested and imprisoned for some political offence. Of his further history we know nothing.

In another town, a father, who was secretly carrying his new-born daughter to be baptized by an Evangelical pastor, was seized and thrown into prison. The poor young mother was dragged from her sick chamber to share the same fate; and eventually both were exiled, and two-thirds of their property confiscated.

In the same town the citizens were driven with threats, or won by deceit, into joining a procession of the Host. John Bleyssa, one of the citizens, firmly refused; and on being asked the reason, replied, " Whenever I have received the holy communion, I have inwardly resolved before God to keep away from this blasphemous ceremony."

"But you will not, surely, oppose the will of the emperor?" rejoined the questioner. "Never, in what concerns the things that are the emperor's," he replied. "But here it is the things that are God's that are in question."

"There may be means found to force you," said the other.

"God," answered Bleyssa, "requires a free-will service, not a service of compulsion."

Bleyssa, for these bold words, had to endure a nine weeks' imprisonment.

His fellow-citizen, John Jahoda, was punished for a similar refusal by an imprisonment, followed by a command to pay a sum of money towards the expenses of a fresh procession and high mass. "I will not contribute to any such ceremony," he said, as he came forward with the money; "for I know of no sacrifice but that of the Lamb slain for the sins of the world, and lifted up on the cross for us. But I pay the money to show my obedience to the powers that be, who may spend it afterwards as they think best."

For this speech he was again imprisoned for a month; and after a second fine had been extorted from him, he was driven from the city with his wife. He died soon after of the plague in Prague, full of faith and peace.

The fate of these confessors was more tolerable than that of many of their countrymen. Numbers of recusants were shut up in noisome dungeons, so close that they could hardly find room to stand; and there they remained, stifled with the poisoned atmosphere and

I

filth, till many died, and others were induced to make some show of submission. Many were kept in towers, cellars, or stables, exposed to bitter cold, hunger, and thirst.

At Prostau many hundreds were shut up in the stable of the castle, every window and aperture being closed. Many fainted from want of air, among others the venerable father of Matthias Ulicky (the pastor whose martyrdom has been already recounted), a patriarch of eighty. He was brought out apparently dead, with several others in the same condition. The brutal captain of the " Reformation Commission" declared " they were only feigning, and must be brought to themselves," and ordered a quantity of cold water to be thrown over them. Some were restored to their senses by this rough means; but the old man expired in the presence of his tormentors. They had done their worst for him; and his happy spirit was released, to join his son in the rest prepared for those who "loved not their lives unto the death," but had witnessed a good confession.

Others were inclosed in cages so narrow as to force them into a painfully cramped posture, which, at the end of two or three hours, became intolerable torture. The nerves were so affected by the strain on the muscles, that the sufferers became almost beside themselves, and were driven in their distraction to say whatever their persecutors desired. Those whose faith was real and earnest afterwards went into exile.

Many entreated on their knees that they might be put to death at once rather than be driven by such misery into violating their consciences; but the reply given was, that the emperor desired not their blood, but the salvation of their souls. Their enemies did not wish that they should have the power of glorying in martyrdom.

And this is the reason why, in the long and terrible persecution which followed the Battle of Weissenberg, comparatively few martyrs can be counted. The will to die for Christ was not wanting; but, in the majority of cases, it was only for political crimes that death was actually inflicted, though the deaths in prison, or from the consequences of torture, must doubtless have been very numerous. The courage and resolution displayed was often quite worthy of the early days of Christian zeal and heroism.

In Prachaticz the imperial army met with actual resistance from the citizens, and one thousand six hundred and sixty of them were slain. The streets were choked with corpses, which lay exposed, often stripped by the soldiers, and for some days none dared to bury them.

At last, two pious sisters, Christina and Benigna Rumpal, buried with their own hands their brother, a citizen of Prague, and their husbands (all of whom had been slain in the encounter), in a grave they had themselves made; and by their words and example of faith and courage led others to follow their example.

A noble lady, Katharina von Loss (she may possibly have been the widow of Otto von Loss, though we are not told so), displayed equal resolution. She would neither give up her faith nor leave her country. " I cannot go into exile," she said, " from want of means; my conscience will not allow me to recant. I will do neither. If they try a third plan with me, they may condemn me if they will; I trust entirely in God."

Strange to say, she was left in peace. Two citizens of distinction maintained the same resolution, and after long imprisonment they were set free.

Four artisans of Koffenburg were kept in prison and exposed to the extreme of cold, hunger, and thirst. At one time they were left utterly without food. A Jesuit visited and threatened them, but Sigmund, one of the artisans, replied, "We would bear all, hunger, the gallows, the scaffold, rather than sin against God. Do what you will," he added, as the Jesuit left him, "only do it quickly!"

But this poor mercy was denied them. For a time they were only supplied' with a small quantity of bread and water twice a-week. Afterwards they were separated and inclosed in different places, one of them actually in a chimney. After twenty-one weeks, in which every effort was made to force them to yield, they were at last dismissed with fines and a sentence of exile. One of them, worn out with hardship and suffering, died on his way.

Another, a clerk, was confined in prison till his feet were covered with the most terrible sores, and rendered utterly useless; but he was filled with such heavenly joy that he spent his whole time in singing psalms and hymns of praise. He died at the end of a year, full of joyful faith and trust; and Huerda, with impotent rage, caused his corpse to be flung over the fortress walls, and buried in the moat by a shepherd.

Such men might well be reckoned among the noble army of martyrs. But, some years after, a humble confessor did actually suffer death by the executioner for preaching the gospel.

In 1629 twenty-two peasants of Zlonic were accused of

having relapsed into heresy after having conformed to the Romish Church. They were led to prison singing hymns of triumph on Christ's resurrection.

Their leader and pastor, George Balthasar, a man of lowly origin and without education, was questioned as to his conduct. He dictated in prison his answer to a secretary, who was employed to write his defence, for it seems doubtful whether he could use a pen himself.

" I have been accused," he said, " of having broken my promise of conforming to Rome, and turning back to the Evangelical faith. My answer is, that I was driven by sufferings during a severe imprisonment to sin against God, my just Judge ; for I had then so weak a faith that I did not believe God could save His own from the hand of man. But I was chastened by Him for my sin, and for a whole year could find no hope in His mercy. At last I remembered the sinners of old time who had repented and found mercy; and I cried to the Lord night and day, and watered my couch with my tears. But our merciful God showed me His loving-kindness, for He wills not the death of a sinner, but that he should be converted and live. I received what I had prayed for ; God sent me His angel, and I saw His glory, brighter than the sun. I was filled at that moment with the Holy Spirit, and I was born again."

He goes on to say that he felt himself called on to speak to others of the truths he had learned. His views seem in some points to have been somewhat fanatical and exaggerated; but that he was an earnest and devoted preacher of the gospel there could be no doubt. He had been preaching for four years, in spite of every effort being made to hinder him; "but the greater the hindrances," he adds, "the more did God strengthen me by His Spirit."

"I came to Zlonic," he continues, with characteristic *naïveté*, "to declare the truth to the people, and call them to repentance, as the Lord had bidden me; and so I did for three days, Friday, Saturday, and Sunday. The last day of the three I had a book with me. ... And it was the will of the Lord they should hear me, for they could not snatch the book out of my hand, though they refused to give God the glory, for I was called to warn them all and exhort them to repentance. . . . Nothing can frighten me; and I have no anxiety, except to fulfil what has been laid on me, and that I will do without hesitation. ... I warn you," he concludes, "not to receive the grace of God in vain, for His rod is already prepared with which He will punish those who will not acknowledge His voice. I have more to say to you; but as I cannot write myself, I must conclude, as I must consider others. But if I can speak openly with you, I shall be able to explain more fully. Meanwhile, the grace of the Lord be with us all. Amen."

The parish priest and several Jesuits came to him after reading this letter, and questioned him further. He owned he was only a layman, and unlearned; but he preached, not of himself, but led by the Holy Spirit. "For," he said, "as I already wrote, I passed a whole year in weeping over my fall; and then the Lord Jesus had compassion on me, and showed me His wounds, which healed the wounds of my conscience. He gave me the light of His Spirit, and commissioned me to speak to others; and what I have done for four years, that I will continue to do as long as I live. I am ready to die for the sake of my Lord Jesus."

In these words he continued to answer his persecutors.   They could only silence him in one way ; and
he was condemned to death. He was brought to Prague,
and beheaded before sunrise, to avoid a concourse of
people ; his body being, as usual, dismembered, and
exposed after death as that of a criminal.

It is remarkable that before his death he spoke in a
kind of spirit of unconscious prophecy.   He declared
that the persecutors of God's people would suffer from
judgments even in this world, and that the scattered
flock of Christ would be again assembled together.   The
persecuted Bohemians recorded instances in which the
first part of this prophecy was verified in the remarkable
judgments which came on several of the leading persecutors.   They also related extraordinary signs, appear-
ances in the heavens, etc., which were said to take place
at the time of these great troubles in Bohemia.   It
would hardly be surprising if the overwrought feelings
of the sufferers had led them to see omens and portents
in simple natural phenomena.   A remarkable burst of
thunder-claps certainly appears to have taken place on
the day when the martyrs of Prague were executed, and
an extraordinary hailstorm on the day of a solemn procession of the Corpus Christi at Kuntenberg, some little
time later.   There were strange stories of fountains of
blood, and other wonders, probably originating in the
excited imagination of the relaters.   Several apostates
were said to have been attacked with furious mania, and
others with fits of the nature of epilepsy ; and other
similar cases are recorded.

It was indeed a day of darkness for Bohemia.   The
rage of the persecutors was not only spent upon men,
but even on the very monuments of the dead.   Graves

were desecrated, bones flung out, monuments in the churches defaced or destroyed. The number of Bibles and Protestant books committed to the flames, or otherwise destroyed, must have been very great. And thus to human eye the Reformation in Bohemia was effectually and finally crushed.

Yet, continues the chronicler, great as the victory of Antichrist appeared, the Church has never been wholly without pious teachers, who openly and secretly, by preaching and writing, strengthened their hearers against future persecution. But it was God's will that, in the general destruction, those who seemed the pillars of the Church should be overthrown. The greater part of the nobility and a considerable number of ministers were scattered and dispersed; and therefore the enemies who had plundered the Lord's heritage rejoiced and triumphed.

But the wrath of man may be made the means of purifying the Church. There was a great sifting among those who professed to belong to Christ, and many were separated who had been united by blood or marriage in the closest ties. Many husbands went into exile whose wives refused to follow them; and many wives for the love of Christ have been compelled to leave their husbands. The persecution was the test which showed what the reality of their faith was. The number of those who preferred banishment to apostasy was very great. In 1630 it was computed that one hundred and eighty-five families of distinction in Bohemia alone, all belonging to the highest classes, had already gone into exile, many of these families numbering from twenty to fifty men; and this did not include the nobility of Moravia, nor the emigrations subsequent to 1630. Above two hundred ministers of the United Brethren were at that time known to have emigrated; and great multitudes of commoners, both from the cities and the country, had even within these first ten years gone into exile. The greater number settled in Saxony; some in Bayreuth, Brandenburg, and even in Holland. Many found a refuge and protection in Poland, Hungary, and Silesia, in spite of the imperial manda e.

Besides the exiles, there were many in Bohemia and Moravia compelled to remain in their country, and who, like the seven thousand of old, would not bow the knee to Baal. Some who were vassals of merciful nobles were protected from severe persecution by their lords, and remained steadfast in the faith. Many, too, are mentioned as being known to the chronicler among those who had been terrified or entrapped into a recantation, who afterwards wept over their fall like Peter, and proved, by the letters they addressed to their exiled ministers, that their repentance was sincere. Some of these were able to reunite themselves to the Evangelical Church, while others awaited, with longing desire, the opportunity to do the same.

"Thou, our God," concludes the chronicler, "look on our misery. We have been brought very low, and are counted as sheep for the slaughter. . . . Comfort us again after the time Thou hast plagued us, and for the years wherein we have suffered adversity. Show Thy servants Thy work, and their children Thy glory. Amen. Amen."

SUPPLEMENTARY CHAPTER.

So ends the Chronicle. But the feelings of lively sympathy, reverence, and admiration for the martyr Church of Bohemia with which we close the record are accompanied by a sense of painfully unsatisfied longing to hear the sequel of the history. We have read of those who died for the faith, and those who emigrated; but what of the multitudes who were compelled by their circumstances or the watchfulness of the government to remain? How was it with them? Did they patiently submit to renounce their faith? or did they keep it in secret? Were there any who, like the "Pitmen" of a century earlier, or the Huguenots of the desert, and the Waldenses of the Alps, met in caves and mountain recesses and forests, to hear and read the Word of God?

The answer to all this—as far as direct information goes—is, at first, apparently, a dead silence. But we have the strongest and most irrefragable evidence that the cause of this silence was not that there was nothing to tell. The Emperor of Austria and his satellites flattered themselves that the outcry against Romish superstitions, which Bohemia had never ceased to utter since the days of Popish usurpation, had been effectually quenched in torrents of blood; but he was mistaken. He had sacrificed the best and noblest men in the country; he had destroyed its prosperity, and changed smiling, flourishing lands into a desert; he had reduced its population to little more than a fourth of what it had been;[1] but he had *not* succeeded in extirpating, as he believed, every trace of heresy from Bohemia.[2]

It is true that, during the second half of the seventeenth century, Bohemia appeared to be, spiritually, a desert. An impenetrable cloud of darkness hung over the land. Still there were, in the midst of this darkness, a faithful remnant of hidden ones. It is very little we can gather respecting them. They had no men like the French Protestants, Antoine Court and his companions, to act as their mouthpieces and draw up chronicles of their history. They had no place of refuge, as the Huguenots had, where their language was spoken, their teachers could be trained, and their records preserved. Their German neighbours in Saxony and Brandenburg could not help them, as French Switzerland could help the French Protestants, for they spoke a different language.

But a few scattered incidents have been gathered here and there, which show us that life was still concealed under the heap of social ruins.[3]

In one village, where a priest and a Romish service had been established in the formerly Evangelical church, the mass was actually celebrated for a whole century in a completely empty church—the priest and his sacristan were literally alone.

[1] From 3,000,000 to about 800,000.
[2] See Appendix, Note C.
[3] For what follows I am chiefly indebted to the substance of a lecture by M. Reichel, the editor of the Moravian publications in French Switzerland. Bost's *History of the Moravians*, published by the Religious Tract Society, may be advantageously consulted by those who wish for further information.

In a parish near the Hungarian frontier, some of the peasants were in the habit of going over into Hungary every Saturday to fetch hay in their carts. The pastor who was to preach to them on the Sunday was concealed in the hay, and thus brought into the village secretly week by week. In another village, a woodman, in his coarse working-dress, with hatchet on his shoulder, might be seen every Sunday passing through the woods, directing his steps to some isolated dwelling. This was another faithful Hungarian pastor, who went weekly, at the risk of his life, to hold a service and preach the gospel on Bohemian soil.

The Bohemians had, indeed, their meetings in the desert, like the Huguenots ; and many retired forests and mountain gorges and caverns echoed the praises of the Lord, even in these darkest times of oppression. Others, less courageous, conformed outwardly to the Romish faith, but read the Bible assiduously in secret, concealing the precious book in a cellar, a hole in the wall, or in a hollow log of wood. Often a father would venture to confide the secret to his children only on his death-bed.

Many held private meetings by night in their own houses. Even among those who had been less tenacious in maintaining their faith, the old habits remained so rooted that the priests were obliged to have recourse to stratagem to reconcile them to the new order of things. One priest found the people so attached to the reception of the cup at the communion that he did not venture to discontinue it at once, but began by giving it in the vestry, then administered it after the service was over, and at last substituted a pot for the chalice !

The attachment to the memory and to the traditional

portrait of John Huss was so great that it was found expedient to carve the statue of St. John Nepomuk with features resembling those of the Bohemian reformer, so as to lead the ignorant insensibly to transfer their allegiance from him to the Romish saint.

But, though the memory of the past was still dear to the Bohemians, the remains of spiritual life were gradually beginning to die away in the country. The members of several families, especially those of Zeisberger, Schneider, Jaeschke, and Nitschmann, had done much to keep alive the faint spark that remained; but after the death of these pious men the outward conformity to Rome became more and more general, and it seemed as if all traces of the ancient and pure Bohemian Church were likely soon to be entirely extinct.

But it was in the midst of this thick darkness that the light was again to spring up. The Old Brethren's Church was to revive again; and, strange to say, it was to be from that poor, hidden remnant of weak and crushed ones who had been apparently cowed into submission to the dominant Church that the new life was to begin. God had indeed chosen the weak, and despised, and helpless, and it might almost be said, in the emphatic language of the apostles—"those who were *not*"—to be the germ of a revived Church, which was to be His instrument in carrying the gospel to the very ends of the earth.

It was in the year 1715 that an awakening began to manifest itself among the scattered remnant in Moravia. Several persons, descendants of the Brethren's Church, in the neighbourhood of Fulneck, Litiz, and other places near, became so anxious for spiritual teaching as to go from time to time to Teschen, fourteen leagues off, to hear the Lutheran preachers there. A pious carpenter, named Christian David, who had been brought up a Roman Catholic, but had been convinced of the errors of the Romish Church, was moved to devote himself to the work of an evangelist, and frequently visited these anxious inquirers. The result was a decided religious revival among them, and they felt, as they became more enlightened and earnest, a strong desire to go to some country where they could worship God according to their conscience.

Christian David, who knew all their difficulties, was acquainted with a pious young "candidate" for the sacred ministry, John Andrew Roth, and through him was introduced to the individual whom God had chosen to be the protector and leader of the little scattered and oppressed flock—Louis, Count Zinzendorf.

This nobleman, who had from early life dedicated himself and all that he had to the Saviour to whom he had given his heart, was deeply moved by Christian David's eloquent and lively description of the neglected and crushed state of his fellow-converts in Moravia. He offered them a temporary asylum on his own estate of Berthelsdorf in Lusatia, near the frontier. The offer was joyfully accepted by two brothers, Augustine and Jacob Neissen, who, with their wives and children, and their cousin Michael Jaeschke, set out at the end of May, 1722, guided by their friend David. They reached their destination in June; and the count's steward assigned them a settlement in a wild forest district at the foot of a hill called " Hutberg."

On the 17th of June they entered on the work of clearing the forest; and Christian David, as he thrust his hatchet into the trunk of a pine, exclaimed, " Here the sparrow has found her a house, and the swallow a nest—Thine altars, O Lord of Hosts!" (Ps. lxxxiv. 3.)

This was the small beginning of the colony which gradually extended, and received the name of *Herrnhut*, or " the Lord's protection." In the course of ten years the little band of immigrants had increased to six hundred souls. The count, with the help of Roth, now the pastor of the flock, was indefatigable in his endeavours to minister to the wants of their souls as well as bodies. They attended the meetings which were held at the Castle of Berthelsdorf.

The congregation increased so much that it was necessary to build a church at Herrnhut. On the 12th of May, 1724, the count and a little band of friends like-minded with himself assembled to lay the first stone of the edifice. At the moment they were so engaged, a party of five young Moravian emigrants, on their way to join some of their brethren in Poland, came up. Struck by the sight of what was passing, they stayed to witness the ceremony, and were so impressed that they determined to give up their intention of going on to Poland, and to remain. The principal of these young men was David Nitschmann, also a carpenter, and destined to be one of the "pillars" of the new spiritual edifice. He and his comrades had come of families who had remained faithfully attached to the old Bohemian Church, and possessed some notions of its discipline and polity. They spoke about it to their new friends, and expressed a wish to establish something of the same kind among themselves. A little later Zinzendorf met with the work of the old chronicler, Bishop Amos Commenius, on the constitution of this ancient Church, and was so struck with what he read that he resolved to re-establish it. He showed the new colonists a translation of the work, and on reading it they agreed to his plan. The discipline and government of the old Brethren's Church were thus restored, and in 1734 the first bishop was consecrated by Jablonsky, grandson of Commenius and bishop of the Brethren in Poland. The first bishop of the new Church was David Nitschmann, the leader of the little company of five who had come to the laying of the church's foundation-stone, and who had already shown his fitness for the office by his zeal, devotedness, and success as a missionary among the heathen slaves in the West Indies. And so the ruined and scattered Church of old Bohemia was again called into life and rebuilt on a firm foundation.

One manifestation of their revived life was exhibited in their missionary zeal. Having acquired a quiet home, a settled organization, and a recognised ministry, they were solicitous to extend to others the privileges they enjoyed. Their chief ambition was to carry the message of salvation by Christ Jesus to heathen lands.

What glorious triumphs the Moravian or United Brethren's Church has achieved for the gospel, in places where at that time little or nothing had been done to make it known, is familiar to us all. We all know how, on the burning plains of Africa and the frozen coasts of Labrador and Greenland, among the Indians and negroes of South Carolina, in the West Indies, and in many other lands, the descendants of the Bohemian Brethren have been and are still faithfully making known the gospel message, with evidences of blessing everywhere; and many are also aware that this Church has been and continues to be the centre of much spiritual life in many parts of Central Europe.

But our object is rather to dwell on the influence it has exerted in Bohemia. To that country Herrnhut and its kindred settlements were as cities of refuge through a great part of the eighteenth century; and during that time a quiet and comparatively unnoticed emigration went on from time to time from Bohemia—among those who still kept the faith in secret, and felt their enforced conformity to the Church of Rome to be intolerable—when once a way of escape was pointed out.

But this exodus was very slow and frequently interrupted, and attended with much peril and anxiety. Little groups of twos and threes moved away quietly and silently, and with much care to avoid suspicion. Then a zealous evangelist would return and bring away one and another of his friends and kinsfolk. Often arrest and years of imprisonment and suffering were the result of his efforts.

The two histories that follow, the most detailed of those we have been able to find among the records of the Brethren's Church, will give some idea of the sufferings, struggles, and difficulties of these confessors.

THE HISTORY OF JOHN GILEK.—John Gilek was member of a family who inhabited the village of Luborg in Bohemia, in the beginning of the eighteenth century. The father of this family was often found by his children engaged in reading by stealth a large book, which he bathed with his tears. He dared not tell them what this book was, for fear of discovery; but he strove to impress their young minds with the leading points of the Evangelical faith; and fearing for them the contact with teachers of a corrupt religion, and other children brought up under its influence, he himself undertook their education.

He did not, however, live to carry it on long; he was removed by death while they were still young, and expired while gazing on the precious book, which he had had brought to his bedside. Doubtless he had committed his dear ones in faith to Him who " giveth the increase."

Of the other children we hear nothing. John, the subject of our narrative, was eleven at the time of his father's death, and had been deeply impressed by his father's teaching. It does not appear whether his mother survived; but the course of the history leads us to believe that our hero was an orphan. Certainly his home was completely broken up, and the poor boy left to make his way almost alone in the world. He was first placed with a distant relation as a farm servant. Here he might have been easily corrupted by the bad example of his companions; but these coarse and profligate men disliked the innocent boy, and made him the object of their scoffs and ill-treatment. Often the poor child bathed with tears the rude couch of hay where he passed his nights in the stable; but he was safer there than in the company of his drunken and profane companions. He " bore the yoke in his youth," and was to find the happy result in after years.

But the time of that blessing for his soul was not yet come. At the age of nineteen he became apprentice to a tailor; his master was a light-minded, irreligious man, who soon led the youth into his own bad courses. But the germ of spiritual life was in his heart. He felt unhappy in his sinful life; and, like the Prodigal Son, he desired to " arise and go to his Father." Of the true way to God through Christ, however, he knew nothing, and his best resolutions were of no effect; still, the Father was "drawing him." One day, taking up a book which described the sufferings and death of Jesus, he was so much moved by the account, and by a picture of the Saviour on the cross, that he could not restrain his tears. An inward voice seemed to say to him, "See what the Lord Jesus endured for you ; and you have neither loved nor thought of Him, but have grieved Him by your sins." This thought took possession of Gilek's soul; he could not rest day nor night ; and in his trouble he consulted those whom he believed to be more enlightened than himself. He applied to a cousin, devoted to the Romish ceremonial, who told him these thoughts were temptations of the devil, and advised him to accompany him on a pilgrimage into Moravia, where he would regain his tranquillity ! Gilek obeyed his blind guide, and performed the pilgrimage, scrupulously observing all the prescribed ceremonies, and even joining a "confraternity" at Brunn. But he returned from his journey more troubled than ever.

A little time afterwards, while working at his trade, he happened to spend some days under the roof of a man whose mind had been enlightened, not only by the knowledge of gospel truth, but by the power of grace in his heart—one of the little flock of hidden ones who had never "bowed the knee to Baal." This good man watched his young inmate attentively, and soon perceived what was going on in his soul. He entered into conversation with Gilek, who soon opened his heart to his new friend. The aged mother of the master of the house took part in this conversation, and related with tears how after the Brethren had been persecuted and driven into exile, she and her companions had met secretly in a private house to read and pray together; how, when they had been discovered and been obliged to leave the house, they had met in the fields outside the village, till at last they had been prevented altogether from meeting, and their Bibles and religious books taken from them by the priests. This simple history recalled to our hero's mind the value his departed father had attached to his books, and the caution with which he used to read them. He began to long to possess these cherished volumes, and concluding that his mother's brother must have kept them, he wrote to him curtly, desiring they might be restored to him. The uncle, alarmed at this letter, thought it prudent to obey. " He has just made a pilgrimage," he thought; " who knows what commands the priest may have laid on him about these books ? If I refuse, I may be denounced."

The books were sent, and Gilek began eagerly to peruse them. The Bible was not among them ; probably it had been seized and burnt long before; but the study of the works which remained to him convinced the young man that his pilgrimage and the ceremonies he had observed since his return were useless. He tore up his pictures of the saints, burned the hymns he had sung in procession, and destroyed his diploma of membership of the sacred confraternity.

Light was beginning to dawn in his mind; but the Bible alone can be the true "lamp to our feet," and Gilek had never even seen one. How was he to procure a copy ? But few of those in Bohemia had escaped the flames, and those few were jealously guarded and concealed by their possessors.

Still Gilek continued to advance in knowledge of the

truth; and those who felt with him were not slow in perceiving this, and were ready to assist him with their affectionate Christian counsels.   Some of these brethren at last lent him a Bible and a hymn-book for a few days.

The young inquirer leaped with joy at the sight, copied about thirty hymns, and, shutting himself into his closet, spent long nights in studying that Word for which his soul was thirsting.   But this study at first only showed him his sinfulness and lost state by nature. His heart, broken and contrite as it now was, had not been able to lay hold of and appropriate the grace so freely offered in Jesus to the sinner.   He sought for peace, and in the hope that he might find it among true Christians, he began to wonder whether there were not in some part of the world men who lived according to Bible precepts.   If he could but find them, he would leave all to live with them, though it were on bread and water!   His friends were able to satisfy his inquiries; they told him that he would find such persons as he sought at Gerlachsheim, in Saxony; that a little while before a family from their village had emigrated thither, and they were expecting a visit from one of the brethren residing there.   Gilek's resolution was taken; he would follow this brother on his return.

But he must first await his arrival; and the waiting time was long and most distressing.   His Romanist neighbours had perceived the change which had taken place in him, and watched him narrowly.   Accusations of heresy and threats of imprisonment were already beginning to be directed against him, when his intended guide arrived.   Not a moment was to be lost.   On the 8th of September, 1731, at nightfall, he left his native village quietly, carrying nothing with him but a little bundle of clothing, and set out with his companion on the road which led to Upper Lusatia. On the fourth day they reached Gerlachsheim in safety.

This place was one of the many in Saxony and Prussia which had offered asylums for the Bohemian immigrants for conscience' sake. A considerable number had already settled there, forming a Bohemian colony and a Protestant Church, under the direction of that excellent pastor Augustine Schulze.

This good man was a faithful shepherd of his flock, and a powerful preacher of Christ crucified. He was not satisfied with a mere assent to the pure teaching of the gospel; he constantly insisted on the necessity of renewal of heart.

"I would not give a farthing for your Christianity," he would often say, "unless you are each individually united closely to the Lord Jesus."

His own simplicity and humility would have made him accept the rebuke even of a child with gratitude; and he constantly encouraged the brethren and sisters of his flock to tell him freely anything of which they disapproved in him, that he might change it.

A congregation, whose members after having preferred the reproach of Christ to all worldly advantages, and become voluntary exiles for His sake, were directed and instructed in the way of salvation by so faithful and so firm a hand as that of their pastor, could scarcely fail to form a Church full of life and energy. Their fellow-countrymen who came to seek the way to pardon and peace among them met with a cordial reception; and the pastor's preaching and the example of the flock bore witness to the free grace of Christ which could not leave the humble, earnest inquirer long in doubt. Gilek was enabled to lay hold of Christ as his Saviour, to receive the pardon and peace which flow from His precious sacrifice, and could soon join with a glad heart in the hymns of praise which continually resounded among the happy Christian band at Gerlachsheim.

But Gilek was not one to rest idly in the enjoyment of his privileges. A truly converted man, like Andrew of old, must be eager to find his brother, and tell him that he has found the Messiah; and in this spirit Gilek felt he could not rest till he had announced the good tidings to his brethren in the flesh, his beloved countrymen in Bohemia. He resolved to make a journey into his native land—at the risk, he well knew, of his life and liberty, for those who attempted to induce professing Romanists to quit their Church and country were liable to the severest penalties; but he went boldly, counting the cost. His journey, through God's mercy, was performed in safety, and his mission greatly blessed. Several of his friends and relations declared themselves ready to leave all to go to Gerlachsheim. A band of twenty emigrants was collected, divided, for safety's sake, into two separate companies. One of these was to set out with Gilek, the other to await his return. The little party travelled by night, through unfrequented paths, hiding by day, in the most secret recesses of the forest and mountains. They would not light a fire to cook themselves food, for fear it should betray them, and could only satisfy their hunger when they happened to pass the abode of some brother in the faith.

The poor fugitives at last reached their destination in safety; but others remained in Bohemia who were anxious to follow; and the indefatigable Gilek set out again on his perilous mission. He was accompanied this time by two friends from Gerlachsheim, and a man from Hennersdoff, who was unknown to him. To please this last, he consented to alter his line of route a little. This, as it turned out, fatal complaisance led them into the neighbourhood of the town of Leutomischl. Here they lay down to rest in a field of new-mown hay, and, exhausted with fatigue, fell asleep. But Gilek's rest was disturbed by a strange dream. He thought he saw the sexton and the Jesuit priest of Leutomischl arriving together to arrest and lead him to prison; and at the same moment he felt some one shake him violently. He awoke with a start, looked round, and saw no one; but a voice within seemed to say, "Depart immediately; make your escape without loss of time!"

He aroused his comrade, and related his dream. The other, wearied and impatient, declared he did not believe in dreams, and must sleep. Gilek was unfortunately persuaded to resist the inward intimation, and, though trembling in every limb, lay down again to rest. But, just as he was falling asleep, he was roused by the arrival of strangers; they were the very persons of whom he had dreamed, the Jesuit and the sexton, who had discovered and come to arrest him; and the two travellers were made prisoners.

It was a moment of bitter anguish to Gilek. He felt that he had disregarded a warning which had been graciously vouchsafed him, and he reproached himself bitterly. And now what sufferings of body and soul lay before him! All were presented to his mind at this moment; and in his agony he asked of himself if he should indeed remain faithful to the truth he had received and the Saviour he had embraced, or be conquered by fear, and perhaps tortures?

But the Lord did not abandon His afflicted servant: these terrible questions were answered by a deep and realizing sense of the value of the gospel of the free grace of God, and a firm assurance that he would be enabled to suffer anything and everything, rather than deny his Saviour.

On the 30th of May, at ten o'clock in the morning, the two fugitives, bound and escorted by a strong guard of peasants, were led into the fortress of Leutomischl. It was no new sight to the inhabitants of the little town; nor did the gloomy prison chambers receive such inmates for the first time. The emigrations for conscience' sake were becoming frequent, and the clergy, supported as usual by the secular arm, were constantly on the watch for families suspected of heresy.

When Gilek first found himself alone in his dungeon, loaded with chains, and his feet in the stocks, he was overwhelmed with the deepest depression. The courage which he had felt on his way to the prison had for the moment failed at the certain prospect of a long captivity, and the probability of a terrible death. The flesh might well quail, for two days and two nights had passed without any food or drink having been brought to him; and it seemed as if his captors intended to starve him to death. The third day he was reduced to a state of extreme weakness; but his soul was again strengthened. He had cried to the Lord, and implored His pardon for all his sins; and He who has said, " Call on Me in the time of trouble, and I will deliver thee," enabled His suffering child to cast himself in full trust upon his heavenly Father.

But his enemies had no intention that he should die of famine. The prolonged fast was intended as a trial of his courage and resolution; and it was at last broken by an additional refinement of cruelty. The jailer entered the prison, and mockingly asking if his captive felt any appetite, he offered him a large piece of bread hot from the oven. The poor prisoner, exhausted with hunger, eagerly devoured the food; and the result of the unwholesome diet after so long a fast was agonizing pain and distress. The next day he was so reduced and prostrated, as to give the persecutors some hope that the weakened frame would react on the mind; and the exhausted sufferer was dragged before the tribunal to undergo his first interrogatory. But he had help of which his torturers knew nothing. He who has said, " My strength is made perfect in weakness," was with him in the judgment-hall, and sustained him during the trying scene. Gilek answered all the questions put to him with firmness, declaring his faith in the Apostles' Creed, at the same time protesting against all the errors into the acceptance of which they tried to entrap him. After a tempest of insults and imprecations, he was taken back to his prison. But he was subjected to a fresh interrogatory the same evening. His judges had sent for two witnesses from his native village, who not only stated that he had conducted a number of persons out of the country, but also brought against him a number of false accusations. In vain Gilek protested his innocence; he was loaded with abuse, and at last, worn out in mind and body, he sunk down in a swoon. As soon as he had been restored by cordials, the judge furiously commanded him to tell the whole truth. The answers did not satisfy him, and the prisoner was sentenced to receive fifty lashes. These were inflicted immediately by a soldier.

The next day Gilek was brought to the town-hall, and questioned by the council. They asked him if he had any cause of complaint against the government, and what were the motives which induced him to emigrate.

Gilek replied that he had no cause of complaint against the count his lord, or against the emperor. He would willingly remain their subject, if he could only be free to live according to his faith and conscience.

They then took pains to prove to him that his faith was erroneous; but, as may be supposed, these efforts produced no effect.

Then they questioned him about a letter they had intercepted, which he had written to an old companion, in which he had expressed a wish that his correspondent might experience the same peace of mind that he himself enjoyed. He was compelled to read this letter aloud, and asked if these were still his views. They were, he replied, and he hoped to remain ever faithful to his convictions.

" A fine preacher," they cried, scoffing, "who does not even know how to write a letter correctly!" And then followed a storm of insults. But in the midst of all this the prisoner's eye caught that of three out of his twelve judges, who, instead of joining the others, were gazing at him with looks of compassion, which seemed to show that they secretly felt with him.

A few days after a fresh occurrence rendered Gilek's position still more distressing. His two companions from Gerlachsheim, who, it may be remembered, had set out separately from him, for greater security, were surprised in the act of escorting some emigrants, and were imprisoned in the same fortress. Gilek was reproached with not having denounced them, and was on the point of being condemned to a hundred blows with a stick; but the Jesuit priest, who was present, objected that the prisoner was too weak to bear them, and he was led back to his prison without further molestation.

Again he was brought to the town-hall, and for half a day every effort was used to bring him to recant; but neither arguments nor threats had any effect on him. He continued calmly to repeat that he would never hear of any means of salvation except through the merits of Jesus.

But about this time an event occurred which gave Gilek some respite. A number of persons, suspected of heresy and intention to emigrate, were arrested and imprisoned. This drew the attention of the judges from Gilek, and for some time he was left in peace. He profited by this period of tranquillity, and spent it in serious reflections, examining his past conduct, and opening his whole heart to his Saviour; and the promised support was abundantly granted. He often enjoyed so sweet a sense of the presence of his invisible Friend, that his heart overflowed with joy, and, like Paul and Silas at Philippi, he made his prison resound with songs of praise and thanksgiving.

But this " time of refreshing " was only the prelude to a period of fiery trial. His tranquillity was first broken by heavy tidings. The news was brought to him that the Elector of Saxony was about to send back all the Bohemian fugitives. The intelligence was false; but he believed it, and was so overwhelmed with grief that for three days he wept incessantly, and was unable to rest.

Then came another messenger of evil tidings. His friend Ostry was also his fellow-prisoner, though in a separate cell; and Gilek knew that he was daily visited by two priests, who held discussions with him for hours, without being able to shake or discomfit him. But at last one of these priests, perhaps with the hope of moving Gilek, announced to him that Ostry had been reconciled to the Church of Rome, and he had better follow his example. Gilek, who loved his friend heartily, and believed him firmer in the faith than himself, was overwhelmed with grief and dismay. The story in fact was false, for the priests, despairing of producing any effect on Ostry, had sent him back to the lord of his native place. But Gilek believed what he had heard; yet in the midst of his deep grief he was enabled to look upwards for help, and to promise the Lord to be faithful to the end; and he felt himself consoled and strengthened from above.

He needed such support, for his trials on all sides increased. He had been seven months in prison, and the severe Bohemian winter was setting in, and was bitterly felt in the chill dungeon where he lay; his clothes were falling into rags, and could hardly protect him against the cold; the bread and water which formed his sole subsistence were often frozen hard; his sufferings were intense; but as long as he rested solely on the Saviour, the power and support given him from above prevented his courage from failing. But one day he ventured to trust in his own strength. Having been taunted with the impossibility of long enduring such a condition, he answered rashly that he would rather die of cold than be overcome. The declaration savoured of presumption, and he was permitted for a time to sink into deep despondency. He prayed earnestly, and confessed his sins to the Saviour; but he still felt forsaken, and the anguish of his soul was inexpressible. His nights were passed in weeping; twice he took no food for three days; he suffered from inflamed eyes, and the cold seemed to pierce him through and through. In the midst of all this mental and physical distress, thoughts of self-destruction were suggested to his mind by the tempter—ever ready to take advantage of human weakness. But the Lord was sustaining him, even while he felt not His presence. A voice within seemed to say, "Do thyself no harm. I have patience with thee, only trust Me." And then once more he could freely pour out his heart to his Saviour, and experience consolation from above. Light and peace were restored to his soul, and even his physical state was relieved; he could breathe more freely, and was again able to sleep.

After Christmas he was moved to a large room which was occasionally warmed. This change appeared at first a great relief; but he soon regretted his solitary cell, for felons were placed with him as his companions, whose profanities and blasphemies distressed his mind more than the cold had done his body.

He was on one occasion in great danger; some soup was brought him, the odour of which was so disgusting as to cause violent sickness. He was unable to touch it, and suspected they had intended to poison him.

Spring came at last, but no liberty for the poor captive. The summer passed, still no change.

In the beginning of the autumn he was removed to a dark, damp, and unwholesome cell, so small that he could not stand upright, and was obliged to remain sitting or lying on his pallet of rotten straw, which was infested with frogs, rats, and other vermin. He was crippled with rheumatism, and shaken with violent fever and ague; again his soul was overpowered with anguish, and he cried mightily to the Saviour; he had lost all confidence in his own strength, and could only exclaim, " Lord, Thou knowest I am lost if Thou dost not come to my help!" The cry was heard. After a sharp conflict of soul he fell into a peaceful sleep; and on awaking he found himself not only free from fever and restored to the use of his limbs but relieved from all mental distress. His heart was filled with peace and joy, and he was again able to raise his voice in joyful hymns of praise.

The needed help had come in time to strengthen him for fresh outward trial. His tormentors appeared to recollect the victim they had nearly forgotten. The Jesuit priest returned to the charge; the Bishop of Choast summoned Gilek before him; he was again brought before the tribunal, and first brilliant promises, and then threats and violence, were employed, in the hope of shaking his firmness.

One night one of his judges entered his cell. " Gilek," he said, "to what Confession do you belong?"

" To the Evangelical Confession, sir," replied the prisoner.

The reply was a blow of the fist on his head, so violent as to fell him to the ground, where he lay stunned for some time. Some blows of a stick at last roused him, and he heard the judge ask him if he would become a Catholic.

" I will not deny my Saviour," was his only answer.

The judge ordered that thirty blows with a rod should be inflicted on the spot. The gaoler was about to execute the order, when the weakness of the prisoner moved even his hard heart. He remarked to the judge that Gilek could not stand upright.

"Well, then, let him lie down to receive them," said the judge.

Gilek prepared to comply; but while doing so he secretly prayed to the Lord. He felt utterly unnerved by the sufferings he had just undergone, and in childlike confidence he told this to the Lord. "Thou seest, my Saviour," he said, "I cannot bear these blows; I shall sink under them." At that moment the judge ordered the sentence to be remitted till the next day. The prayer had been heard "while he was yet speaking." For seven consecutive nights the implacable judge came to renew his threats, and each time went away baffled by the imperturbable calmness and resolution of the prisoner. A strength not his own had been given him.

One day, as he was returning from an examination in which the most frightful threats had been addressed to him, to break what they called his obstinacy, he was followed by one of the youngest councillors, who whispered to him, "Fear nothing; you have done no harm; they only want to frighten you." These words encouraged him greatly; and the next time he was brought before the council he spoke freely of having left Bohemia in order to worship according to his conscience, and that he was determined to remain faithful to the Evangelical faith, according to the dictates of that conscience, whatever might be the consequences. A little time afterwards he was summoned to the presence of the governor of the fortress, a man of whose violence of temper he had often heard. He went in much anxiety, and praying the Lord to help him. The governor was in company with a Jesuit, and both seemed resolved to make a great effort.

"Are you Gilek of Luborg?" the officer began. Gilek assented.

"John Gilek," he resumed, after a pause, "would you persevere in holding your faith, even if perpetual imprisonment, the gibbet, or the stake, should be your punishment?"

The question was repeated three times, solemnly and deliberately: and three times Gilek replied, with unshaken firmness,

"Yes."

Then the governor, turning to the Jesuit, said, "I can do nothing more with this man; he is right, after all, in saying what he thinks; others say they will conform to the Church, and do not really do it after all."

With these words he dismissed the prisoner, send ng him some assistance afterwards.

One morning, near Christmas, Gilek was informed that he was to be publicly excommunicated. At eight o'clock he was taken to the church, and placed in the middle of a circle including the magistrates and clergy. The Jesuit, coming forward, declared that the obstinate and blinded heretic must be publicly excluded from the only true Church, and declared unworthy of the merits and intercession of the saints. He abandoned him, as he said, to the evil one and to hell. Gilek commended himself, body, soul, and spirit, to his Saviour, and remained calm and immoveable in the midst of the threats, anathemas, and looks of horror of all around him.

After the ceremony, which seemed to be a mere empty form, the priests returned to the charge, and

L

exhorted the man they had just delivered over to perdition to confess to them, promising, with a show of friendship, to procure him all kinds of favours if he would but abjure, and to keep his secret faithfully if he had any murder to acknowledge.

Gilek, smiling, begged them not to be troubled on his account, for his rejection by their Church gave him no uneasiness.

His sentence was declared next day : he was condemned to labour in chains at the public works in the town. He was set immediately to break the ice in a cistern ; but he was so reduced by his sufferings that he could scarcely lift the hatchet. He was surrounded by a crowd of curious spectators, some insulting and mocking him, but others showing marks of sympathy.

From this time he was employed in cleaning the streets of the city, his left hand chained to his right foot. It would appear that the life in the open air restored his strength, which must originally have been great; and it is evident that the life of a convict labourer, however hard, was tolerable in comparison with his existence in prison. When employed in cleaning the courts of private houses, he was brought into communication with several kind-hearted persons, whose sympathy and benevolence probably considerably softened his captivity.

About a year and a half had passed in this manner, when one morning in the year 1735, while he was employed in his usual work, he was startled by the sound of the alarm-bell. A fire had broken out in Leutomischl : thick clouds of smoke were rising, and the whole town was in confusion.

At first, Gilek's only thought was how best to help others. Observing that the flames threatened the house of an old woman who had constantly shown him kindness, he hastened there, and finding his benefactress ill in bed, he succeeded in carrying her through the crowd to a place of safety. He was returning to the scene of conflagration when another acquaintance of his begged him to lead his cow out of the city. Gilek did so, and then, for the first time, it occurred to him to consider if he might lawfully avail himself of the opportunity of making his escape. He tied the cow to a tree, and then lay down near it, praying earnestly that the Lord would show him what he ought to do.

" If no one comes to look for me till the evening," he thought, " I will look on it as an indication that I may escape."

He lay still and waited; one and another passed by, but no one noticed him. When it was quite dark, he tried to break his chain with two large stones, and, wonderful to relate, succeeded. Tears of joy flowed from his eyes when he felt his chains drop off. He threw himself on his knees to thank God, and then proceeded towards the forest, through which he walked the whole night.

At last fatigue and hunger made him slacken his pace, and towards morning he entered a solitary inn. The innkeeper and his wife were startled at the arrival of a man with disordered dress and hair, without coat or shoes. But Gilek related the history of the fire, and this drew their attention from his person. He took something to eat, and then penetrated again into the forest, where he continued his march for two days, taking the direction of the frontier.

At length he reached the mountains of the Saxon Switzerland, over which he must pass to reach Saxony. Exhausted with fatigue, hunger, and anxiety, he painfully toiled up the steep pass, leaning on two sticks. The fourth day of his journey, he reached the top of the mountain pass by midnight; he found a spring, at which he quenched his thirst, and then, wearied out, he threw himself down on the soft green moss which carpeted the forest, and slept profoundly. But in a moment he awoke with a start; it seemed to him that some one was rousing him. He looked round and saw two wolves moving towards him!

Alone, without means of defence, in the recesses of the forest, he saw the glaring eyes fixed on him in the darkness, and even his stout heart was ready to sink. He trembled in every limb; but he remained motionless, and prayed earnestly to his Saviour not to allow him to perish by so terrible a death. And marvellously was his prayer answered. The wolves appeared about to spring on him; but, as if their hind feet had been nailed to the ground, they remained immoveable, in the posture of attack, but did not come nearer. Gilek redoubled his prayer, and suddenly the two savage beasts turned and fled. We may imagine his joyful gratitude to his Almighty Deliverer. Strengthened and encouraged, the poor traveller passed the frontier, and six days after he had left his prison arrived happily at Gerlachsheim, where he was received with joy and thankfulness by all.

The Bohemian colony was, however, obliged soon after to leave this peaceful asylum. The Saxon government was alarmed by the complaints and threats of Austria, on account of the continual stream of emigration; and the fugitives at Gerlachsheim, availing themselves of the hospitality of Prussia, established themselves, some at Berlin, and some at Rixdorf, in its neighbourhood, where they formed churches on the model of the Ancient Brethren's Church at Bohemia, like that which had been already established at Herrnhut.

Our hero joined the Bohemian Church in Berlin, and devoted himself to labour in this new field as heartily as his strength, reduced by long years of suffering, would permit. He gave himself principally, as he had done at Gerlachsheim, to the instruction of youth; and in this occupation he quietly passed the remainder of his life, never showing any self-exaltation on account of his past sufferings, but walking humbly with his God as a pardoned sinner depending solely on Him. At the age of seventy-three he expired, bearing witness to the last to his firm dependence on the merits of Jesus Christ.

HISTORY OF ROSALIE LINHARDT.—The next history we shall relate gives the account of the escape of a family of secret adherents of the gospel in Bohemia, drawn from the autobiography of one of its members, and affords us another glimpse into the difficulties with which the Bohemians still attached to the gospel doctrines had to contend.

Rosalie Linhardt, the daughter of a prosperous miller of Dragonitz, in Bohemia, was born in May, 1745, and brought up by devout Romanist parents in the strictest practice of their religion. From an early age she seems to have been under serious impressions, and to have sought God earnestly according to her light.

At the age of sixteen she was married to a man named George Herodez, who carried on a respectable business as a baker, and whose father had been one of the magistrates of the town where he lived. Soon after her betrothal, the young bride was alarmed by hearing from the priests that her husband's family had long been suspected of heresy. She readily promised she would warn her spiritual advisers as soon as she perceived any signs of the latent poison she had been taught to dread.

But a year passed before anything occurred to rouse her fear. Her husband was kind and indulgent, and wisely left her at first to follow her own devotions unmolested, being probably aware that a premature expression of his own sentiments might close the door permanently to any prospect of influencing his wife.

Her confessor and some of his fellow priests came one day to pay the young people a visit; and something, either in their manner or conversation, seems to have shaken for the first time Rosalie's entire confidence in them. She expressed this to her husband. He then let her further into the light of the real character of those whom she had thought so saintly, and who were really far from being "faithful shepherds." This led to fuller confidence between herself and her husband; his arguments gradually convinced her of the falsity of the so-called miracles wrought by images, etc., and the uselessness of the rosary and similar observances.

She gave up her stated prayers with the rosary; but the old habits had not lost their power. She became very unhappy, and reproached her husband for persuading her to renounce what had been such a comfort to her. "What happy moments I have lost!" she cried. "My child," said her husband, tenderly, "it is written,

'Pray without ceasing.'" But this could not satisfy her. She returned to her old devotions continually ; and he had the patience and good sense not to urge her to desist.

But an incident now occurred which led her to clearer views. Her father-in-law, who seems to have been an enlightened Bible Christian, came to see them one day, and taking the New Testament read to her the passage in John x., "I am the door of the sheep," etc. He then asked her if she thought we might come to Jesus just as we are. "Yes," she replied ; "but still, if we visit a great lord we must be introduced, and so it must be with the Lord Jesus." The good old man explained to his daughter-in-law that the Saviour was not like an earthly magnate, but was willing to receive us just as we are, and that we need no other intercessor with our Heavenly Father. His words made a strong impression on his young hearer, and from that time she seems to have embraced the faith of the gospel with heart and soul.

She now joined the little meetings of gospel Christians who gathered together secretly at her father-in-law's house for Bible readings and prayer, and felt the blessing and advantage of this Christian communion. The old Herodez had preserved a Bible and several valuable religious books, which he had inherited from his ancestors of the old Brethren's Church. He was a firm adherent to their doctrines, and kept the faith, and sought to edify others in secret.

But this could not last long. The unsleeping eye of the Romish power was upon them. The priests began to watch more carefully for suspected heretics ; and their attention was awakened by observing that the wife of young Herodez, who had been formerly so devout a Romanist, had ceased to bring offerings and kneel before

the shrine of the Virgin. Father Wenzel, who seems
to have been her confessor, made a pointed allusion on
one occasion in his sermon to one who *had* been a pious
Christian before her marriage, but had now joined the
heretics.

A traitor, too, was in the camp. A cousin of George
Herodez, a man named Noach, was persuaded by his
wife to betray his own father to the authorities, in order
to get possession of his property. The old man, who
was eighty years of age, was accused by his son and
daughter-in-law of possessing Lutheran books, and not
fasting on Friday; and on the strength of this depo-
sition he was seized and thrown into prison. But this
was only the beginning of troubles. Noach never rested
till he had betrayed all whom he knew to entertain
Evangelical views; and Rosalie's father-in-law, the elder
Herodez, was thrown into an underground dungeon,
with hands and feet chained, in company with his aged
colleague Noach.

Much attention was excited by this. The people
naturally inquired why a man generally respected, who
had been burgomaster for twenty years, should be imprisoned and manacled like a common convict; and the
answer to all questions was, "He is a heretic!" His
son dared not move in the affair, for fear of being seized
and forced into the army. All therefore devolved on
his wife and mother, who undertook to have the prisoner's
cause pleaded; and Rosalie, fearless in the strength of
her new faith, was indefatigable in her exertions.
Friends were raised up, who secretly assisted them;
among others, Rosalie's uncle, the Dean of Gutemberg.
With the help of these friends, a memorial was drawn
up and laid before the Consistory at Prague. But the

matter remained long pending, and the devoted young daughter-in-law was involved in her father-in-law's disgrace.   Her own father and mother and other relations were forbidden to speak or eat with her because she was a heretic; and as they obeyed these commands strictly, she was entirely isolated from her family.

"This did not prevent me," she writes, "from visiting my father-in-law daily in prison, and conversing with him in the presence of his jailer.   On account of these visits I was cited before the Consistory, examined closely by the priests, and then handed over to the secular arm.   They treated me very roughly; but the Lord gave me strength to persevere."

She was to have been put under arrest immediately; but the delicate state of her health induced her persecutors to allow her to return home for the night.   "I went," she says, "to my husband, and we passed the whole night in prayer to the Lord Jesus to assist and deliver us."

Next day she was again examined for several hours; and in answering the questions put to her she was sensible of the support and presence of the Saviour. She was to have been placed in the pillory, and a number of boys were prepared to pelt her with mud; but she was released, on the same ground as before. While she was undergoing examination before the judges, her husband's young brother, a child eight years old, was questioned in the next room, and actually beaten severely with rods, to make him confess that his mother and sister had Lutheran books and sang Lutheran hymns.   The courageous little fellow endured the pain without making any disclosure, only crying out in his agony, "Lord Jesus!"

"Little rascal!" cried his tormentors. "Why don't you cry 'Ave-Maria,' or 'Jesus-Maria!'" Wearied out with his firmness, they at last dismissed him.

Meantime the old burgomaster remained in his prison, and his son and daughter-in-law were harassed with incessant annoyances and persecutions. One night the little family were surprised by a visit from their father. He had been allowed by the jailer, an old soldier who had known and esteemed many of the Lutherans, and was well-disposed to them, to come on parole, to warn his wife and children that a party of forty men were coming next day to search the house for Lutheran books, and that any who should find a single line of these books would receive ten crowns as a reward.

"No words," continued the narrator, "can express our terror. We hastened to heat the stove and burn all our books, with many tears. My father-in-law returned to his prison, and we waited trembling for the morning. As soon as it was light the inquisitors arrived, and, finding nothing, they were in a great rage. One place, however, still remained to be searched—the loft—which was full of corn, among which we had ventured to leave a few books in hiding. But the mercy of God caused a heavy rain to fall, and inspired us with courage to say that if they brought out our corn and exposed it to the rain, they must pay us beforehand for the damage done to it. Being unable to pay, they ceased their search, and, apparently suspecting nothing, retired ashamed of their ill-success. The evening of the same day our father was liberated."

But their troubles did not end here. The priests threatened them continually, questioning all who had visited the house, in hopes of being able again to denounce the

suspected family. They lived in perpetual terror. In
the midst of all this distress a son was born, who did
not long survive his birth. The poor young mother
became dangerously ill, and hoped for a speedy removal
to the presence of her Saviour.

But He had another lot in store for her. She gradually
recovered ; and the efforts of their enemies to betray them
were all, by the merciful care of God, defeated. No one
would declare anything against them ; and after three
years of anxiety, many fresh interrogatories, and innumerable difficulties, the cause which had been pleaded
so long before the government was declared in their
favour, and they were proclaimed innocent. Their
enemies were strictly forbidden to molest them, and their
relations were allowed to renew their intercourse with
them. The priests treated them with apparent kindness;
but they dared not trust them, knowing themselves, in
spite of all apparent friendliness, to be strictly watched ;
they therefore gave up holding meetings, and contented
themselves with reading the Word of God in private.
The father died about this time, in full faith, exhorting
his children to hold fast to the Saviour to the end.

The persecuted family spent some years in peace.
But meantime the young brother who had been so bold a
witness for the truth had gone to work at his trade at
Olmütz, and there had heard so much of the Brethren's
Church, that he returned home, declaring his intention
of going himself to seek out these people, and ascertain
if the reports he heard of them were true. He went
accordingly to Berlin, was invited to Herrnhut, and
obtained leave to remain there. He wrote to his family,
telling them of all he had seen and heard ; and they
endeavoured to carry out the principles of the Church of

the Brethren in their lives, especially in withdrawing from worldly gaieties.

Rosalie lost her father soon after this. He had attached himself particularly to his Protestant son-in-law; and Herodez and his wife had the comfort of being able to console their father's dying hours with words of gospel truth, and seeing him depart in the faith. From this time all the desires of the husband and wife pointed to Herrnhut. George Herodez went at last to visit the Church there, and returned home determined to leave all to join those with whom he could worship in spirit and truth. His wife entirely agreed with him; and they were purposing to set forth, when the illness of Herodez put a stop to their plans. An accidental hurt he had received on his journey, followed by an attack of fever, brought him to the grave at the age of thirty-three. Four days before his death he took a tender leave of his wife, and asked her what she thought of doing after his decease. She promised him that she and her two surviving children (they had lost four by death) would leave all and go to Herrnhut. He was rejoiced at this, but was anxious as to her means of doing so. "The Lord Jesus will send me a travelling companion," she replied; "and He is with me Himself."

George departed in peace with the joyful hope of being reunited to his dear ones before the throne of God. The young widow was left in deep grief and much perplexity. For a woman with young children to make such a journey alone was impossible; and in her case the strictest secrecy was essential, if she would carry out her plan. She could only commit herself to God, and await His leading. Some time afterwards she had a visit from a man who brought greetings from her brother-in-law at

Herrnhut, and an invitation to visit him there. She was at first afraid to trust the stranger, but finding he had been her husband's guide to Herrnhut, she begged him to return to ask her brother-in-law's help in forwarding her plans. He soon returned with encouraging messages from the younger Herodez, and advice to take with her all the property she could. She began to sell her goods, but soon found this gave rise to remarks, and she was obliged to desist. Fresh trials now assailed her. Her brother-in-law, from some unexplained cause, took fright, and consulted friends who were against the plan. One wrote to her that, as she *could* be saved in Bohemia, she ought to remain there.

All this harassed her greatly ; but she still felt she ought to remove to a country where she had liberty of conscience, and could bring up her children in the truth. She sent for a M. Roth, a pious friend, to whom she opened her mind, and who encouraged her, if she felt she was really actuated by a desire for spiritual advantages, to persevere.

But her family and friends were not idle on their side. A highly advantageous second marriage was proposed to her, which would have placed her in affluence, if she remained ; while in leaving Bohemia she and her children were in danger of actual want. The pain of leaving country, family, and friends, and the dread of the evils in prospect, weighed on her, and she was almost shaken, for a moment, in her resolution. She at length mentioned the subject to her eldest child, a little girl of seven years, to whom she had often talked of Herrnhut.

" My child," she said, " would you be willing to give away your toys to the children here, and come to Herrnhut ? "

"Yes, mother," said the little one.

"But if they were to put me in prison for trying to go?" asked the mother.

"I would go and beg with my sister," said the child, "and bring you something to eat in prison."

These simple words moved the mother to tears; she was ashamed to see that her child had more trust than she had herself; and, remembering her promise to her husband, she resolved to depart. She arranged her affairs as well as she could without attracting attention, placing the proceeds of her sales in the hands of M. Roth till she could claim them. Then she spoke to a "messenger" to procure her a carriage for the journey. "I rely on you entirely," she said to him. "No," he replied; "do not rely on me, but on the Lord Jesus, who alone can help us." These words, showing his Christian faith, cheered the poor lonely young widow.

She now proceeded every night to pack up in *feathers* a portion of the necessaries and valuables she wished to take; as feathers were at the time a considerable article of export from Bohemia to Saxony: when all was done, the packages were transferred secretly to an inn about half a league off.

On Palm Sunday, March, 1774, she put off her mourning and went to church, to escape all suspicion; then paid a visit to her relations, and, as she says, bade them adieu in spirit, as she dared not declare her intentions. Next day, when out, she met Father Joseph, a priest she knew, who asked if she still thought of going to Saxony. Her heart beat with terror, but she turned it off as if playfully, by saying, "To be sure; why not? Come with me to-night, and carry one of the children for me!" He thought she was in jest, and said no more.

That night, at eleven o'clock, all those living near who were secretly gospel Christians met in the young widow's house, and united with her in prayer for God's protection in her perilous undertaking. "We separated," she says, "feeling that my fate would either be a happy refuge in the Brethren's Church, or else imprisonment and martyrdom." This was the alternative before her. She "counted the cost," and set her face resolutely towards the Promised Land of the Bohemian Protestants.

With her two little girls, she then abandoned her house, and garden, and fixed property, and set out with her friendly messenger and her brother-in-law, who seems to have joined her. The little party walked to the inn where the luggage was awaiting them; the carriage was prepared, and, with the good wishes and prayers of the friendly landlord, they set forth. They soon reached the banks of the Elbe; but the boatmen were asleep, and for some time could not be roused. The poor fugitives were in much anxiety and alarm; however, they succeeded in passing the river before it was light, and reached Bobwitz, their first halting-place, where they were received by secret gospel Christians, but had to be concealed in the loft, because the master of the house, being accused of having Lutheran books, was expecting every moment to be taken to prison.

The mother and her little ones were obliged to remain in this hiding-place two days and two nights, before another carriage and driver could be procured. On the 31st of March they proceeded to a shepherd's cottage, the last place in Bohemia where they met some who were secretly gospel Christians. Here they left their luggage till it could be sent for, and proceeded on foot through a thick forest, in heavy rain, and over a ground slippery with ice, on which the elder girl stumbled and fell many times ; the younger was carried by her uncle. As they approached the frontier, the messenger forbade them to speak, for fear of drawing the attention of the hussars who were on guard. The darkness was intense, and the poor wearied travellers had to walk in this way for several leagues, till at last they reached a farm in a deep valley, in which they passed the rest of the night.

The next day was Good Friday. The brother-in-law returned to the shepherd's hut in a carriage to fetch the luggage, on pretext of bringing feathers to sell at the market of Zittau. To keep up this appearance, a messenger went to Zittau to engage a woman to come to meet the carriage at a neighbouring village and take the feathers, as if to sell.

The fugitives meanwhile had to remain alone in the farm, where they were treated with much kindness by the good people. The day was passed in anxiously awaiting the return of her friends. It was not till eleven at night that the messenger came with the woman he had engaged ; and the brother-in-law and the carriage did not arrive till next morning. When the driver saw the two children and their mother, he at first refused to go further ; and it was only by much persuasion and double payment that he could be induced to go on. The brother, with the woman who was to personate the saleswoman, proceeded in the carriage with the packages, while Rosalie and her children continued their route on foot, under the guidance of the messenger. Still further to elude suspicion, he made them part company when they reached a point nearer the frontier, and, taking one path himself, directed the mother and children to take another. The paths met at last, and having engaged a girl to carry the wearied little ones by turns, they passed the frontier.

Rosalie continues: "When the messenger said, 'There, we are now in Saxony,' I was overpowered with unspeakable joy. My children rejoiced with me, and we together thanked and praised the mercy of our Saviour, and sang aloud hymns of praise for His help in bringing us in safety. After taking some refreshment, we continued our route, and reached Zittau in the evening. But the carriage was not there, though I thought I had seen it on the way. I went into the house where we had intended to lodge, and, retiring to my room, thanked the Lord for His wonderful deliverance, praying Him to bring our companions in safety, even though my property should be lost; for I felt such a sense of His presence that I could have resigned myself to lose all. As I came downstairs I saw the carriage stop at the door. I shed many tears of joy and gratitude at this relief."

On this, the night of Easter Eve, the poor mother and her little ones were able to sleep in beds for the first time for a week. On Easter Day she went to the Bohemian church, and for the first time enjoyed the blessing of hearing a Protestant sermon. In the evening a man came to tell her that the woman who was to take charge of her goods would be put in prison if thirty florins were not paid. She, of course, readily gave them, ill as they could be spared, and afterwards learned that she had been the victim of a sharper's trick.

At Zittau she met several persons who had had business relations with her father, and who were astonished that

M

one belonging to a family of such zealous Romanists should have been able to leave the country ; they tried to persuade her to stay at Zittau, promising to show her every attention. But the noise and confusion which she heard from the people arriving from the public-house, on Sunday night, etc., disgusted her so that she would not remain another day at Zittau, and next morning, leaving her children at their temporary lodging-place, set off with the messenger-guide for Herrnhut. They arrived before noon, and the guide went immediately to greet her brother-in-law, who replied, " She has thought better of it, no doubt, and will not come."

" She is at the door," replied the guide. The brother could only thank God for His mercies to the forlorn widow. She was brought to a house near the church, where a Brother who knew Bohemian came to speak to her, and told her to wait some days, till she could know if she might remain.

" Oh ! " she replied, " I can't wait. My husband told me to come to Herrnhut. I am here, and must stay."

When her visitor had left her, she went to her room, and prayed earnestly that the hearts of the Brethren might be made willing to receive her. The prayer was answered, and she met with a warm welcome.

Next morning she returned to Zittau, where she found her two little ones clinging to each other, crying and sobbing, in terror lest their mother should not return to them. They were too early used to hear of terrible family tragedies. But when she appeared and answered to them that they were " going to Herrnhut," the joy of the little ones, who had been taught to look upon it as a " Land of Canaan," was great.

The little family settled among the Brethren. Rosalie

at first was hindered by her ignorance of German, which her children, as generally happens, learnt more quickly than she did; but she appears to have gradually become " naturalised," and two years later was re-married to Martin Schön, a member of the Church. Her second marriage was a happy one, though it only lasted eleven years, when she again became a widow. She took part in the superintendence of the " Widows' house," at Nisky, another settlement of the Moravians, and appears to have spent the remainder of her life in active Christian usefulness and peace. Her two daughters were both married to missionaries, and she herself died at an advanced age, universally esteemed and respected.

But meanwhile a dawn of better things was opening in Bohemia itself. In 1781 the Emperor Joseph proclaimed liberty of worship in his own states. A very limited and scant liberty it was, clogged with innumerable restrictions; still it was permission for the Protestants of the empire to exist. In many places, in the Salzburg country in particular, where the gospel Christians had suffered greatly, and been banished by thousands, this permission called into life churches where nothing like Protestantism had been suspected, and still more was this the case in Bohemia. Protestant parishes rose up as if by magic in the midst of the country supposed to be completely won to Rome. There were seven villages around Königsgratz alone, and many more elsewhere, whose inhabitants in a body declared that they had remained Protestant in heart during more than a century, although submitting outwardly to Rome, and that they eagerly hailed the opportunity of confessing their faith openly. The choice was only between the Lutheran and Reformed Churches; the Brethren's Church was out of the question. Still, for these poor long-oppressed people, it seemed an emancipation.[1]

It was not, however, till after 1861 that full liberty of worship was accorded.

And now, in our days, what answer can be made to the question as to the present state of Bohemia? The first view we might take of the country would not be altogether a cheering one. Bohemia has been made, thanks to the policy of the Emperor Ferdinand, a very decidedly Romanist country.

Whereas before the great battle of the White Mountain, which crushed Bohemian liberties, there was only one Romanist for every thirty-nine Protestants in the whole country, *now* there is only one Protestant to be found for forty-nine Romanists. There are now about a hundred Protestant congregations scattered over the country, chiefly in the places which were formerly the centres of the old Brethren's Church; but these are hardly more numerous than the Romish Churches in Prague alone.

And even regarded as a pious Romanist might regard them, the state of the Bohemian people is anything but an encouraging one. A system of forced conversions is little likely to train up even a religious and moral Romanist people. The moral corruption is very deep and general, and scepticism not less so. The once generous and high-spirited people are now chiefly enthusiastic in the pursuit of amusements, and those often of a kind neither ennobling nor favourable to morality. They

Forty parishes were of the Reformed Church, and twenty Lutheran.

have been kept for centuries in ignorance and mental subjection, and the corrupt tree is bearing its poisonous fruits. Superstition has produced, as it constantly does, unbelief; and infidel works are widely spread in the country where three centuries ago the works of the great Reformers were welcomed eagerly.

So far, it is a dark picture ; but it has its bright side. There is still a strong national sentiment in Bohemia ; and though at this moment the general fermentation of the public mind is rather political than religious, this feeling may easily be brought to bear upon questions connected with religious reformation. A commemoration of John Huss was, it is well known, enthusiastically celebrated a few years back. His portrait, with those of Commenius and Ziska, may be found in almost every house. Romanists as well as Protestants are zealous in their efforts to disinter the volumes buried or hidden by their fathers ; and these books are now republished and read with avidity.

In 1848, the Confession of the Ancient Church in 1574 was brought out with this remarkable title : " The Spiritual Diamond of Bohemia, lost since the battle of the White Mountain in 1620, and found again after 228 years."

Since the increased liberties were granted, a few years ago, there has been a considerable religious awakening in the country, especially in the north-east.

In 1868, a peasant of the village of Lukawick, being anxious for instruction in the gospel, set out in search of a Protestant whom he heard of as living in the neighbourhood. On the pretext of selling his corn, he went from house to house till he found the person he was in search of, who seems to have been an enlightened

and pious man.   They had a conversation which lasted
for hours, and the inquirer returned home the joyful
possessor of a Bible.   He soon gathered round him a
little company of persons anxious about their souls,
and who met to read the precious volume ; and when a
Moravian evangelist came to the village, he found a
room set apart for the service, and a numerous and
attentive congregation.

Similar incidents occurred elsewhere.   A desire was
felt for the Word of God, and this prepared the way
for the gospel teachers who were to follow.   When
once the country was thrown open to Christian work,
the Moravian Brethren felt that no place could have a
stronger claim on them than the spot which had been
the cradle of their Church.

One of their first stations was Rosendorf, a village
a few leagues from the frontier.   It had formerly been
one of the parishes of the Ancient Brethren's Church ;
and the faith had been kept in secret during the long
years of despotism and intolerance.   The little company
of believers held their service in retired nooks among
the mountains, where they read together their sole Bible,
the only one which had escaped destruction, and which
was carefully treasured and deeply venerated.   Later,
when more liberty was allowed, they ventured to meet
at the house of a peasant named Guth ; their numbers
were small, but these few humble Christians were so
full of zeal and desire for spiritual food, that they often
walked to Herrnhut, a distance of from eight to ten
leagues, to hear a gospel sermon, or to be present at
some religious festival.   They were in their turn visited
by evangelists of Herrnhut ; but they longed for a chapel
and a pastor.   They named their wish to the Herrnhut

brethren, and their request was heartily responded to. In 1864, the chapel was built, and the Pastor Beck, from Herrnhut, was installed as preacher. Fortunately, it had been built on a more spacious scale than would have been required by the original flock, for Sunday after Sunday every vacant place was filled by eager Roman Catholic hearers. "We will only come," they said, "as long as the sermons are so good." "But hitherto," adds the narrator, "they have vainly expected the bad sermons, and the good ones have produced their fruit!" In the first year of his ministry, Pastor Beck admitted twenty-six Romanists into the Protestant Church; and the work has gone on steadily ever since.

Nor are these hopeful signs limited to Rosendorf; a similar awakening is perceptible in the whole of that district of Bohemia which borders on Silesia and Moravia, the ancient cradle of the faith, which has often been called the Cevennes of Bohemia.

Since 1868, the most oppressive laws against the Protestants have all been abrogated, and the work of evangelization has made greater progress. Many evangelistic agencies have been at work to spread the word of God through the country, and to help in the establishment of schools and the training of teachers.

Within the last ten years, a remarkable instrument of good has been raised up in the person of John Hattwig. He is a convert from Romanism, a man in humble life, without learning, and not originally speaking Bohemian; but his lively faith and untiring energy seem to supply the place of earthly helpers. By earnest prayer and diligence he has acquired fluency in the Bohemian language; his simple, joyful, childlike faith seem to triumph over all obstacles, and his labours are truly apostolic.

During the war of 1866, the priests arrested him as a Prussian spy, and he was seized and marched off at the point of the bayonet by a guard of four soldiers. Far from being dismayed, he was rejoiced at the opportunity of speaking to his escort of Christ, which he did till he was brought before the commandant of the prison.

" It is quite true," he replied, calmly, when questioned by the officers. " I am a spy; but my business is to betray the kingdom of Satan, and contribute to the victory of Christ's kingdom. As to the political affairs of this world, I know nothing, and wish to hear nothing, of them." He was at once released, and returned nothing daunted to his peaceful conquests.

Several times his quiet self-possession and courage have defeated the efforts of those who have come to seize him or to interrupt the meetings he held. One day, when they were singing the concluding hymn at a service, a blacksmith of herculean strength, of well-known and ferocious character, entered the room. He could hardly have appeared there with peaceable intentions. " But," says Hattwig, " fearing some violence, I had begun the meeting with praying the Lord to protect and guard us, and send His angels to watch the house. And He did so; the man could not come till all was over, and when the worshippers dispersed he remained sitting on a bench as if he expected another sermon from me. I did not wait to be asked. I pointed out to him that he was the wretched slave of his evil passions, and was rushing on like an unreasoning brute, to a career which must end in destruction. He evidently had not expected this attack, but he seemed as if chained to the spot; and when at last he rose to go he made many apologies for having come. I replied, that there was no need for apology, and that he would always be welcome whenever a sermon was to be delivered in this place." Hattwig continues in "labours abundant," and is now the superintendent of an orphanage of which he was himself the founder.

In another part of those mountainous and forest-covered tracts in which the early Brethren of Bohemia used to meet and worship, a revival has taken place within the last six or seven years. The awakened ones had been for some time previously in the habit of paying an occasional visit to Herrnhut for instruction and spiritual refreshment; and one of these men, having a brother in the village of Zebus, frequently spoke to him during his visits of what was so deeply absorbing his own attention, and brought him a Bible. The brother was awakened by the perusal of the book; the flame spread; and soon a little band of converts was found in the village. When they heard that a pastor (employed by the Free Church of Scotland) was to preach at a town five leagues off, they set out on foot to hear him, and begged that they also might be visited. Their request was granted. About this time, the Pastor Schubert had been asked to preach at the adjoining village of Brotzen. A room was engaged; but the difficulty was that there were no resident Protestants at Brotzen; and the Austrian law did not permit any celebration of Evangelical worship unless some of that communion were residing on the spot. The pastor and his friends consulted the carter who was to drive them over. "I have long," he said, "been intending to embrace the Evangelical faith openly. I am a Protestant at heart, and will be so in reality from this day."

Thus the village of Brotzen was opened to the pastor. But the inhabitants of Zebus also were anxious to be present at the service; while the priests were determined to prevent their attendance. "The sermon shall be stopped, if it is to cost me my life!" cried the curate of Brotzen.

The appointed day came. The scattered Protestants of the neighbourhood hastened to Brotzen, and crowds of Roman Catholics from all the neighbouring villages joined the throng. The priest met them at the entrance of Brotzen, and tried to turn them back, but in vain. All thronged to the room which had been engaged. It was locked; the priest had bribed the Jewish landlord with a large sum to return the payment he had received, and to refuse the use of his room. What was to be done? The benches were flung into the street, and the crowd was waiting outside. The carter's room was too small to hold the tenth part of those who had come. A neighbour consented to lend his large court; all was arranged in a short time for the preaching, and the pastor was anxiously watched for. He arrived, but was met by a summons to present himself before the mayor; he went, accompanied by the friendly driver.

"Sir," said the mayor, "I cannot authorize your preaching here, as the village does not contain a single inhabitant who professes your religion."

"Pardon me, sir," said the driver, "I am a man of the Evangelical Church." The mayor was astonished;

but he had nothing to reply, and the pastor and his friend repaired to the court where his congregation was awaiting him.

He was about to begin when a fresh interruption occurred : the préfet of the district arrived, and desired the pastor to stop. " You have asked for authority to preach in a *covered* place, not in the open air," he said. " Your service is no concern of the Catholics, and the driver's room will more than hold the few Protestants."

This was a new difficulty. But another neighbour came forward and offered the use of his room, which was a spacious one. The benches were brought, the windows and doors remained open; and when the room was full about 2,000 remained at the entrance to listen. Three times the Romanists were ordered by the préfet to disperse, the gendarme trying to enforce the command with the butt of his gun ; but all in vain, no one would stir; and to avoid a tumult he thought it best to yield. Then orders were given to shut doors and windows ; but the pastor interfered, and represented that this was to outstep the limits of authority, that the master of the house had a right to keep his windows open, and that he himself intended to preach so as to be heard by all. Then he proceeded to preach the gospel earnestly and forcibly. After the service was over all dispersed peaceably ; but on all sides the remark was heard—

" We never heard anything like this before !"

The préfet himself, who had listened attentively, went to the mayor, and told him he would do well to come and hear the next Protestant sermon ; for himself, he owned he had never heard so good a one in his life.

A fortnight later the same pastor preached at Zebus to a multitude of most attentive Roman Catholic auditors; and in the autumn of the same year, a Moravian pastor in the employment of the Free Church of Scotland was established at Brotzen. The first regular service was on the anniversary of the commencement of the German Reformation, and Luther's famous hymn, "Eine feste Burg," was sung. Since then (the account was drawn up in 1870) twenty-eight men and women had joined the Evangelical Church.

Recent accounts all show that the work is spreading, quietly but steadily, in many parts of the country. At Czaslau, the scene of so much persecution in the days of the Emperor Ferdinand, a new Protestant church and minister's house were erected on the day of the second centenary of Huss's martyrdom. It has been determined to commence a seminary for training Evangelical teachers in that city; and it is likely to be a considerable centre of evangelization.

We hear of gospel preaching and attentive audiences in that very Leitmeritz where so many died for the faith in the early days of the Bohemian Church; and evangelists are at work in many parts of Bohemia and Moravia.

We may take comfort, then, in the hope that He whose ear is open to the prayer of His faithful servants is answering the petitions poured forth in prisons and on scaffolds two centuries ago, and does indeed already "look down, and behold and visit this vine," which will yet bring forth fruit to His glory.

APPENDIX.

―――◆―――

NOTE A.

Milicz, a Moravian of Crenisier, was the Archdeacon of Prague, and Secretary to the Emperor Charles IV., who was also the King of Bohemia.   In 1364 he actually resigned his large emoluments, in order to devote himself entirely to the spiritual good of others.   For several years he acted as an itinerant preacher, earnestly pressing heart-repentance on his hearers.   At first his influence was impaired by the strangeness of his accent, or his Moravian dialect; but eventually his preaching made a deep impression.   One of his disciples, in a memoir written of him, relates that many of his female auditors, who had taken pride in the luxury and magnificence of their dress, began to lay aside their lofty head-dresses studded with gems, and dresses adorned with gold and silver.

He was more and more convinced that the Church had sunk into the grasp of Antichrist.   He treated on this topic in St. Peter's at Rome in 1367, but was silenced by the Inquisition.   Urban V., however, who was just endeavouring to re-occupy the old metropolis, released the culprit from his chains and sent him back to Prague.   He there resumed his work; but certain friars, envious of his popularity and writhing under his rebukes, commenced a fresh attack on him. He expired at Avignon in 1374, while the judicial process they had instituted was still pending. One of his contemporaries was an Austrian, Conrad of Waldhausen, who adopted a like method in Vienna for awakening all classes of society. He was at length invited by the Emperor Charles IV. to aid the holy movement in Bohemia; and the sermons which he there delivered seemed to have produced a marvellous effect. Like Milicz, he proved himself particularly obnoxious to the mendicants, who strove to silence him. Their opposition failed, however, and he died in peace in 1369. . . . . He is sometimes called "Von Stickner," through an error of the press, which confounded him with another of the same class.—Hardwicke's *History of the Church of the Middle Ages.*

NOTE B.

Among the numerous followers of Milicz, none acquired so high a reputation as Matthias of Janow. . . . In 1381 he was collated to a stall in the cathedral church of Prague. The scandals there laid open to his gaze impelled him to rebuke the monks and clerics, in a work *On the Abomination of Desolation in the Church.* A more important work, however, is entitled *Rules of the Old and New Testament,* in which he handles the corruptions of the age with terrible severity. Among the remedies on which both he and Milicz had insisted was a greater frequency in the reception of the Lord's Supper; but a synod held in Prague in 1388 discontinued the practice by forbidding laymen to communicate more than once a month. — Hardwicke's *Church of the Middle Ages.*

In his long-lost work, *De Regalis,* Matthias thus repudiates tradition :

"The Lord Jesus did not give any written law to His followers, although He might have done this in His lifetime in many ways, but merely placed His own good Spirit and the Spirit of His Father in the hearts of believers for a living and perfect law, and a generally sufficient rule of life. . . . . Wherefore, too, His apostles, desiring not to burden the people believing in Jesus with various doctrines, inventions, and precepts, wrote few things, commanded still fewer, and confirmed unshakeably by statutes fewest of all. . . . . Whence it appears that those later persons have acted, and still act, cruelly and coarsely, who have introduced, and authoritatively confirmed, their numerous inventions, various doctrines, and rigid commands. . . . . So that there is such a multiplicity, and so infinite a multitude, of such doctrines, and inventions, and commandments of men, that they have filled many books, and those very large and costly ones, which no one hardly but a rich man could procure ; nor even if he devoted himself to them throughout the whole of his life could he sufficiently read and beneficially digest them."—Pattison's *History of Evangelical Christianity.*

NOTE C.

The noble foundation laid by Huss in Bohemia was eminently successful. But, unhappily, the profession of Evangelical dogma became allied to political Protestantism, and suffered eclipse when the latter was extinguished at the battle of Weissenberg (the White Mountain) on the 8th of March, 1620. The nationality and religion of Bohemia were totally suppressed. The emperor's triumph was consolidated by persecution on the one hand, and by the efforts of the Jesuits on the other. The Slavonic (Slavonian) language was superseded by the German. Dr. Milman says, " Bohemia, as a province of the Christian world in insurrection against the unity of the Church, was even more beyond the pale of mercy than a heathen land."

The lonely believer could only hold his tenets in secrecy.

Yet there were many who sympathised with the individual feeling expressed by Johann Heertman in 1630 :

> " Say, wherefore thus by woes wast thou surrounded ?
> Ah ! Lord ! for my transgression Thou wast wounded.
> God took the guilt from me, who should have paid it ;
> On Thee He laid it."

Recent events have restored religious freedom and a measure of nationality to these countries ; and one unexpected result has been that the gospel messenger, in penetrating the outlying districts with the Word of God, has come on proofs of the continuance of Evangelical light during all these dark ages, and of the existence of individuals and small communities holding fast the profession of Evangelical doctrine under the ban of the law. The following are extracts from the reports of the British and Foreign Bible Society, 1870–1871, concerning colportage in Southern Austria.

"In one place (our colporteur) met with a small company of believers, who, hidden from the eyes of the multitude, and deprived of the ordinary means of grace, have for years upheld a clear testimony of Christ's finished work in the midst of much surrounding darkness ; with the help of some precious books, they and their fathers had retained the gospel in their neighbourhood from generation to generation. Some of these books . . . were two hundred years old. . . . ."—Pattison's *Evangelical Christianity.*

NOTE D.[1]

Confessions of the Church of the United Brethren of Bohemia, Moravia, and Poland.

It is remarkable that this comparatively small Church published, during the one hundred and sixty years of her existence (from 1457 to 1617), no fewer than nearly sixty

---

[1] For this abstract of the Confession of Faith of the United Brethren, I am indebted to the valuable assistance of the Rev. A. Hassè, a leading member of this Church.

different editions of her creed. Of these, twenty differed considerably, both as to form and contents. Some of these have been lost. Dr. Anthony Gindely, in his *History of the Bohemian Brethren* (Prague, 1857 and 1858, two vols.), enumerates thirty-four as more specially entitled to the name of " Confessions."

Many reasons may be advanced for this extraordinary literary activity. Conscious of their integrity, the Brethren were anxious to defend themselves against the many calumnies hurled against them. Then, again, it was necessary to prepare editions, not only in Bohemian, but also in German and Latin. Changes took place so rapidly in the circumstances of the Church, that these versions of the original documents underwent various alterations, till they came to be looked on as distinct productions. And, thirdly, their doctrinal views were modified by their increasing diligence in the study of God's Word and progress in understanding it; and after 1517 the influence of the Protestant reformers is clearly discernible.

The following remarks have reference to the chief Confessions, as enumerated in a list given in an essay of the Brethren's bishops written in 1572 (Cröger's *History of the Ancient Brethren's Church*, vol. i., p. 86).

I. Presented in 1467 to Rokycana and George Podiebrad, King of Bohemia. The following occurs in this first Confession :

" He who has right, true, and living faith has also power to mortify all evil in himself. Whoso appropriates Christ's merits, obtains through Him forgiveness of sins, and thereby the power of His resurrection ; so that he loves Him, cleaves to Him, and becomes thus a new creature through the seed of the Divine Word. But all outward righteousness and good works, done according to the mind of the flesh, are unavailing to salvation, for the childlike spirit is wanting."

Further, they warn against danger of a man's deceiving

himself or the people by speaking of the appropriation of the merits of Christ without having the true Spirit of God, and thus abiding in the old Adam, in the sinful life of the world. They say, if any one asks concerning extraordinary revelations made to them, he is to be told that they regard the greatest revelation to consist in the conviction, in the Spirit, of the truth as it is in Christ Jesus, and of this being the earnest of their salvation. They declare it must not be supposed that they condemned all who did not hold to them. Whoso kept to Christ in living faith would be saved, to whatever Church he belonged. With all such they wished to stand in the unity of the Spirit.

II. Confession of 1468 (or, according to Dr. Gindely, 1470). This Confession was presented to King George Podiebrad and the Bohemian Diet. So the Brethren write: "We inform your majesty that we purpose to bring forward distinct, indubitable passages of Scripture given us by God, to prove (especially if there should be a council of the whole Christian Church) that men do right to withdraw from the obedience claimed by the Romish Church; that the authority of the popes is not grounded on the power of the Spirit of God— thus their blessing or curse derives no power from the power of Christ and His apostles; that their rule is, on the contrary, an abomination before God; that they do not possess the keys of discernment between good and evil, nor the power to bind and loose. The same holds good of the popish legates, who tread in the footsteps of the popes, and walk in their spirit."

III. The third Confession (fourth and fifth of Gindely) appeared in 1504, and has fourteen articles. In the introduction, the Brethren, on the sole ground of Holy Scripture, profess adherence to the Apostles' Creed, as also to the creeds of Nicæa and of Athanasius.

"1. Of God the Father," it is said, "we believe that He in mercy gave to the world for its redemption and salvation,

His only Son, begotten from all eternity, through whose merit the only Father works salvation according to the purpose of His election. We believe in the Father when we accept His testimony from heaven concerning His dear Son. We believe on God the Father when we heartily love Him, the Almighty Creator of heaven and earth, and when we, according to knowledge and ability in our deeds, keep His commandments.

"2. Of Christ, we believe that He is the only true God, equal to the Father and the Holy Ghost in essence, power, and wisdom, even proceeding from the Father, and who also made the world. That He might fulfil the promise of the Father, He descended from heaven for the salvation of men, partook of human nature, was seen on earth by the eyes of men, was cruelly nailed to the cross, and breathed out His soul along with His innocent blood ; on the third day He was again awakened from the placid slumber of the grave, and after forty days was borne aloft in a luminous cloud. He is seated at the right hand of the Father, as a faithful messenger on the throne of grace, advocating those who have received the heritage of glory. He never more forsakes His Church ; all creatures are subjected to Him, and confess that He is Lord. When He descends again, all His enemies shall be subject to Him. We believe in Christ when we own the truth of all His commandments, which require from us faith, trust, and love towards Him. We believe on Him when we own Him to be our God and Saviour, receive all His words with full confidence, embrace Him with undivided love, and are united to His true members in faith and love.

"3. Concerning the Holy Ghost, we believe that He is only true God with the Father and the only begotten Word, and proceeds from both. Through His gift of faith, whereby He quickens, renews, and changes, every believer attains to the participation of the meritorious grace, the justification, the truth, the strength, and complete redemption of Christ.

By Him every believer attains to the participation of the meritorious grace, the justification, the truth, the strength, and the complete redemption of Christ. By Him the holy Church is firmly established, just as He also purifies, justifies, sanctifies, governs, gathers, strengthens, and renders faithful every member in the true faith. The Holy Scriptures have been inspired by the Spirit ; and it is through Him that men understand them. By Him the members of the Church are united. From Him proceed the gifts for the government of the Church, and all that belongs to the life of glory. We confide in the Holy Ghost when we give full assent to the Holy Scriptures. We believe in the Holy Ghost when we, with a clear understanding, love Him in faith unfeigned, and preserve till the heavenly glory all His revelations in fellowship with those members on whom He has breathed.

" 4. We believe in one Holy Catholic Church, the gathering of all Christians called of God and enlightened by the Holy Ghost ; outside of which there is no salvation, and in which there is no condemned soul, the true Church. The visible Church contains men evil and good. We do not announce ourselves to be the true Church, but we strive to become members of it through the profession of, and obedience to, the truth. We have chosen the narrow, painful, and reviled road which Christ Himself, the Saviour and also the Church, His bride, condemned and rejected by the world, walking in the footsteps of Christ, has trodden. We do this rather than desire the enjoyment and the pursuit for a season of the lusts of the world."

It is clear that the Brethren laid the chief stress on the essentials of Christianity, viz., the grace of God in Christ, and the acceptance of this grace through faith ; and further, that there is no trace of belief in the efficacy of the sacraments in themselves, by mere outward participation ; but that, on the contrary, repentance and forgiveness of sins, with faith, love, and hope, as well as the following after Christ, are demanded. The Brethren draw a clear line of distinction between living faith, on the one hand, and dead knowledge and mere literal orthodoxy on the other. Further, they ground all doctrine on the Word of God, as contained in the Holy Scriptures. The teaching of these Bohemian Brethren, already, before Luther's Reformation, may therefore in its essential points be termed Evangelical, though it still needed purification. Of this the teachers of the unity were subsequently well aware, as is proved by later Confessions.

IV. The Confession of 1508, as drawn up by Lucas of Prague. Here, testimony is specially borne against purgatory as a human invention, and not as a scriptural doctrine. It is affirmed that Christ has obtained the purification from sins by His blood, and that therewith is closely connected the right knowledge of grace, of repentance, faith, love, and hope. The separation from the Romish Church is also justified by the testimonies borne to the corruptions which existed within her pale ; such, for instance, as were referred to in the writings of St. Bernard and the Italian poet, Petrarch.

V. The fifth Confession (or ninth of Gindely) was that of 1525, which was presented to King Lewis. It contains the reasons, and the history, of the Brethren's separation from the Romish Church, with the declaration that the Brethren, as Bohemian Christians, had been constrained for their salvation's sake to establish a distinct community.

VI. The sixth Confession was issued in 1532, and drawn up by John Huss, perhaps aided by John Augusta. As the first announcement of the Brethren's doctrines after the German Reformation, it shows the influence of that work. It was translated into German, and presented to George, Margrave of Brandenburg, to whom the education of King Lewis had been intrusted. This document contains a distinct statement of the doctrines of repentance and of faith in the gospel, with forgiveness of sins for him who with true repentance believes the word. Hence arises a new covenant of man with God, and this covenant leads to a justification of the sinner, and a new obedience (*i.e.* the walking according to the Spirit, Rom. viii.). Whoso abides in this covenant is prepared to good works, *i.e.* the fulfilling of the commands of God ; this is the duty of a pardoned sinner ; but it affords no righteousness before God, still less can the sinner's guilt be thereby removed. But the believer receives the armour of God, *i.e.* the strength of the inward man for the contest against the devil, the world, and his own flesh. The victory in this contest arises from firm faith in Christ, notwithstanding the sinfulness which still cleaves to us. In perseverance to the end are to be found our blessedness here below and our hope of eternal life.

During the intercourse of the Brethren with Luther and the other Reformers, both German and Swiss, several new and revised editions of former Confessions appeared. One of these was printed at Wittenberg in 1738, under Luther's auspices, and with a preface from his pen.

Gindely states that the Confession of 1564 was a *new document*, and was drawn up by Peter Herbert. It was translated into German and presented to the Emperor Maximilian. The same writer says this Confession differed materially from that of 1535, especially regarding the doctrine of the Lord's Supper.

It is this Confession of 1564 which Peter Hall, in his *Summary of the Protestant Confessions* (London, 1842) speaks of as the "Confession of 1573." But Dr. Gindely declares that the edition of the last-named year was only his German translation of the edition of 1564 (originally written in Bohemian). Hall gives the contents of the twenty chapters, or at least, extracts of the articles.

The copy of the edition of 1573 presented to the Emperor Maximilian in 1575 was signed by seventeen noblemen and one hundred and forty-one knights, who were all members of the Brethren's Church.

HISTORICAL WORKS

PUBLISHED BY THE

RELIGIOUS TRACT SOCIETY.

————⌇⌇————

THE HISTORY OF ENGLAND. From the Invasion of Julius Cæsar to the Year 1852. By the Rev. THOMAS MILNER, A.M. 12mo. Two Maps. 5s. cloth boards.

THE HISTORY OF GREECE. For use in Schools and Colleges. By the Rev. F. ARNOLD, B.A. Map and Engravings. Crown 8vo. 6s. boards.

THE HISTORY OF ROME. Three Maps. 12mo. 3s. boards.

HISTORY OF THE CHURCH OF CHRIST. In 6 vols. 12mo. 18s. cloth boards.

ANCIENT EGYPT. By Rev. G. TREVOR, M.A., Canon of York. Fcap. 8vo. Map. 4s. cloth boards.

EGYPT: FROM THE CONQUEST OF ALEXANDER THE GREAT TO NAPOLEON BUONAPARTE. By Rev. G. TREVOR, M.A. Map. Fcap. 8vo. 5s. cloth boards.

THE COUNCIL OF TRENT. 18mo. 1s. 6d. boards; 2s. half-bound; 4s. 6d. morocco.

THE DAYS OF QUEEN MARY; OR, ANNALS OF HER REIGN. Engravings. 12mo. 3s. boards; 4s. half-bound. Cheap Edition, 1s. in paper cover.

THE LOLLARDS. Engravings. 12mo. 3s. cloth boards; 4s. half-bound.

THE HISTORY OF THE REFORMATION. By DR. MERLE D'AUBIGNE. Post 8vo. Edition, in five vols., 20s. boards; may be had separately. Cheap Edition, in one large vol., 8s. boards. Quarto Edition, with steel engravings, 21s. boards.

HOW I CAME OUT FROM ROME. An Autobiography. By C. L. TRIVIER. Translated from the French. Crown 8vo. 3s. cloth boards.

THE JESUITS. A Historical Sketch; with the Bull of Clement XIV. for the Suppression of the Order. By the Rev. R. DEMAUS, M.A., author of "Hugh Latimer," "William Tyndale," etc. Demy 8vo. 1s. in cover.

INDIA: A HISTORICAL SKETCH. By Rev. G. TREVOR, M.A. Map. Fcap. 8vo. 3s. cloth boards ; 3s. 6d. extra boards, gilt edges.

INDIA: ITS NATIVES AND MISSIONS. By Rev. G. TREVOR, M.A. 3s. cloth boards ; 3s. 6d. extra boards, gilt edges.

HISTORY OF THE MACEDONIANS. Medium 8vo. 2s. cover.

HISTORY OF THE MINOR KINGDOMS. Super-royal 8vo. 2s. cover.

HISTORY OF THE MORAVIANS. By A. BOST. Fcap. 8vo. 3s. 6d. boards.

ROME AND ITS PAPAL RULERS: From the Fall of the Western Empire. By the Rev. GEORGE TREVOR, M.A. 8vo. 8s. cloth boards.

RUSSIA, ANCIENT AND MODERN. By the Rev. GEORGE TREVOR, M.A. Fcap. 8vo. Map. 4s. cloth boards.

THE SPANISH PENINSULA. Fcap. 8vo. Maps. 3s. cloth boards.

A HISTORY OF THE VAUDOIS CHURCH TO THE PRESENT DAY. By ANTOINE MONASTIER, Pastor in the Canton de Vaud. 12mo. Map. 3s. 6d. cloth boards ; 5s. half-bound ; 7s. morocco.

THE AWAKENING OF ITALY AND THE CRISIS OF ROME. By the Rev. J. A. WYLIE, LL.D., author of "The Papacy." Crown 8vo. 5s. 6d. bevelled boards.

FOOTSTEPS OF THE REFORMERS IN FOREIGN LANDS. Eight Coloured Engravings. Fcap. 8vo. 3s. 6d. boards ; 4s. extra boards, gilt edges.

THE MADEIRA PERSECUTIONS. By the Rev. W. CARUS WILSON, M.A. Royal 18mo. 1s. 6d. cloth boards.

MEMORIALS OF THE ENGLISH MARTYRS. By the Rev. C. B. TAYLER, M.A. New and Revised Edition. Engravings. Medium 8vo. 7s. 6d. extra boards.

THE REFORMATION IN EUROPE. 18mo. 1s. 6d. boards ; 2s. 6d. half-bound.

THE WILL-FORGERS: OR, THE CHURCH OF ROME. By Rev. C. B TAYLER, M.A. 18mo. 1s. cloth boards.

www.ingramcontent.com/pod-product-compliance
Lightning Source LLC
Chambersburg PA
CBHW031109020726
47495CB00007B/2112